WADSWORTH PHILOSOPHERS SERIES

ON

DESCARTES

Garrett Thomson
College of Wooster

Wadsworth
Thomson Learning

Australia • Canada • Mexico • Singapore • Spain
United Kingdom • United States

Printed in the United States of America
    3 4 5 6 7 03

For permission to use material from this text, contact us:
Web: http://www.thomsonrights.com
Fax: 1-800-730-2215
Phone: 1-800-730-2214

For more information, contact:
Wadsworth/Thomson Learning, Inc.
10 Davis Drive
Belmont, CA 94002-3098
USA
http://www.wadsworth.com

ISBN: 0-534-57593-5

CONTENTS

PREFACE

Descartes changed our conception of the world. He was a visionary thinker who was the first to have the idea of understanding all physical changes with a few basic laws. He applied this powerful idea to an enormously wide range of physical phenomena from astronomy to anatomy. He ground lenses, observed stars, cut up carcasses, experimented with magnets, and he read, thought, and wrote to bring together knowledge into a unified whole.

Descartes also worked on the methodological and philosophical implications of this new science. As a young man he was first and foremost a mathematician and, based on his own mathematical experience, he developed a practical method of investigation and general problem solving. Towards the middle of his life he tried to unveil the philosophy of his project. His Method of Doubt was a revolutionary idea that helped liberate generations of thinkers from the confines of Medieval Christian thought. Yet he also helped make it possible for science and religion to coexist. Descartes remained a Catholic all his life and argued that the new science was compatible with the important teachings of the Church.

In all this Descartes articulated changes which other thinkers were also feeling. Europe was undergoing a profound revolution that resulted in the birth of science. Each epoch has its own assumptions that most thinkers of the time can hardly articulate, let alone critically examine. Descartes had an amazingly creative mind and was able to challenge the ruling view of the universe and of human life of his time. This book is the story of the unfolding of that creativity.

I would like to dedicate this book to my father, Alan, who started me thinking about Philosophy and Descartes, by asking me as a child, how I knew that I existed.

1

Preface

This book owes a lot to many other books written on Descartes. I would like to single out Stephen Gaukroger's, Descartes: An Intellectual Biography. I would like to thank Dan Kolak for all his help.

References to Descartes' texts are usually to the standard complete works, edited by Charles Adams and Paul Tannery in eleven volumes. The citations will appear in this form: AT V 28. Other collections of Descartes' work use this form of reference

1
Context

On the 21st August 1609, Galileo gave the first ever public demonstration of the telescope. The invited Venetian officials climbed the tower of St. Mark's cathedral. They gasped with amazement. They could see ships that could not be spotted with the naked eye. This first telescope could magnify only ten times. A few months later, Galileo made one with a magnification of a thousand. He turned it to the night sky. It was his turn to be astounded. He saw a universe utterly different from anything ever seen before. The sky was full of stars (ten times as many as are visible to the naked eye). The Milky Way was a huge cluster of stars. There were mountains on the moon. Within a year, Galileo discovered four of the moons of Jupiter. Furthermore, he was able to confirm Copernicus' theory that the planets revolved around the sun. Copernicus had challenged the traditional belief that the planets and stars revolved around the Earth, which was assumed to be the center of the universe. This traditional conception had been previously sanctioned by the authority of scripture, Aristotle and St. Thomas Aquinas. Galileo observed the phases of the planet Venus, which were explicable only on the assumption that it went around the Sun and not the Earth.

These were such powerful discoveries, so challenging to Medieval ways, that the professors at Padua University refused to even look through the telescope at the night sky. After a long period of inquisition, on June 22, 1633, Galileo was found guilty of heresy and disobedience to the Church for treating Copernicus' claims as a proven fact. Galileo was imprisoned. Remember that in 1600, when Descartes was four years old, the Church had burned the philosopher Giodarno Bruno for his heretical views.

The news of Galileo's imprisonment seriously affected Descartes; he decided to refrain from publishing the book he was writing. In a letter to his friend Mersenne he wrote:

> This has so strongly affected me that I have almost resolved to burn all my manuscript, or at least to show it to no-one..

The whole Modern period was an extraordinary drama, a huge struggle between two world views: the emerging Modern science and Medieval religious and scholastic thought. The outer aspect of the story tells of the diminishing power of the Church as a political institution. The inner story tells of the conceptual revolution which made contemporary society possible. Ultimately, it is the conceptual revolution which interests us most, for Descartes had a vital role in it.

Historical Background

There are some important landmarks in the slow outer political revolution. The first is the invention of the printing press. As more and cheaper books became available, more people outside church institutions became interested in knowledge. A European community of free thinkers emerged slowly and they corresponded with each other.

The second landmark came on October 31, 1517, when Luther nailed his 95 theses to the door of a church in Wittenburg. He was scandalized by the indulgences being sold by the Church to raise funds to complete the new building of St. Peters. At first, he campaigned publicly for Church reform. His work was printed and read widely in Germany. Finally, Luther gave up the idea of reforming the Catholic Church from within, and set up a new church, which led to the proliferation of Protestant Christian sects around Europe.

The third landmark was the greater separation of the state from the Church, especially in Northern Europe. During the Medieval period the Church was the most powerful and wealthy institution in Europe. The Pope appointed and dismissed kings and Emperors. The Church taxed nations for the crusades, for its own buildings and administration. After Luther, many northern European states became independent of the Roman Church, and the new Protestant churches were in a subordinate position to the state. For example, in 1531 Henry VIII established the Church of England. Just as Guttenberg's press made Luther possible, Luther made Henry VIII possible.

These outer changes went hand in glove with a profound transformation in peoples' conceptions of the universe. During the Medieval period, only a very small minority of people had access to learning, and in most of Europe, this was exclusively through the Church. The general Medieval picture of the universe changed little for centuries. The Earth was seen as the flat center of the universe, around which there are seven spheres or domes. The universe was seen as made up of the four elements: earth, water, air and fire.

The Church worried about any deviations from authorized belief. In part, this was a genuine concern that free thinking would undermine faith and lead more people to damnation. It actively discouraged free learning. In 1586, the Jesuits issued the following statement of doctrine: "In logic, natural philosophy, ethics and metaphysics Aristotle's doctrine is to be followed." A Jesuit circular also proclaimed: "Let no-one introduce any new opinion in philosophy and theology without consulting the Superior or Prefect...Let all professors conform to these prescriptions...This is not just an admonition, but a teaching which we impose."[1] Investigation consisted in studying the Bible or the classical texts of Aristotle or those of St. Thomas Aquinas. Debate consisted in citing and making deductions from such texts. Descartes himself studied in a Jesuit College. Despite maintaining a loyalty to the Jesuits all his life, he was a spearhead in the changes which ultimately destroyed this closed-mindedness.

The changes which swept Europe originated in the rich culture of the Arabs. Their ideas spread through Europe, because of their presence in Spain and Sicily and because of the Crusades. For example, paper came to Europe from China through the Arabs. It is found in Mecca in 707, in Egypt in 800, in Spain in 959, in Sicily in 1102, in Italy in 1154, in Germany in 1228, and in England in 1309.[2] Among other things, the Arabs brought the culture of ancient Greece back to Europe. Early Medieval Europe was unfamiliar with the varied culture of Greece. In particular the works of Aristotle were unknown and when they were translated into Latin, they fueled a mini-Renaissance in the 12th century. The scientific works of Aristotle, and those of the Arabic thinkers, Avicenna and Averroes, emphasized the importance of observation, experiment and logical argument. These works opposed the abstract speculation of the earlier Roman-Platonic tradition.

Because of the extraordinary mind of St. Thomas Aquinas (1226-

1274) the church was able to harness Aristotle and turn him into orthodoxy. In the 13th century Aristotle's works became the common texts for teaching philosophy, with emphasis on instruction in formalized logical arguments. Aquinas tried to reconcile the revelations of Christianity with the earthly knowledge of Aristotle and attempted to show that theological claims are consistent with the demands of reason. His *Summa Theologica* became the main textbook for instruction in theology. Thomas's version of Aristotle became the new dogma.

Throughout the 15th and 16th centuries, rational thought became more independent of Christianity. Philosophy separated itself from theology. Europe became wealthier. A new middle class developed which included professionals devoted to learning outside ecclesiastical institutions. Furthermore, the Renaissance in Italy caused a huge increase in translations of classical Greek works. Society became familiar with Greek drama, poetry, and history. The arts flourished. There was a new confidence in the air and a new desire for learning.

By the end of the 16th century the conditions were ripe for a revolutionary change. The modern era was about to be born. Modern science and philosophy began to replace Aristotelian scholasticism . Probably the three people most important in causing these changes were Galileo, Francis Bacon and Descartes.

The Slow Birth of Science

What was the conflict between the Church and Galileo really about? Looking back, it seems strange that the Church should insist that a stationary Earth. Why dig your heels in here?

At one level the conflict was really about authority. Up to the late 16th century a common form of scholarly argument was to amass relevant supportive quotations and references from authoritative sources, such as the texts of Aristotle and the Bible. The Church decided issues based on the authority of its tradition. However, the emerging new sciences, such as astronomy, had no place for arguments from authority. They relied on observation and reasoning. The English philosopher Francis Bacon argued strongly against authority based arguments. The new science required freedom from such authority to investigate the universe without prejudice and superstition.

However, authority was only part of the conflict. The whole picture of the universe and of human existence was at stake. According to the traditional Christian view, the universe was a quasi-organic piece of handiwork created by God full of omens and signs. Modern science was beginning to paint an entirely different picture. It seemed to portray the universe as completely material and all changes as mechanical. Such a picture of the universe had no place for the soul nor for God, and thus threatened to make religion redundant. The stakes were high.

We should understand the modern challenge to the Church and scholastic tradition as a dispute about the nature of explanation. How can natural phenomena be explained? The traditional answer was based on Aristotle's four types of causes: material, formal, efficient and final. We can explain an object in terms of:

   a) its material cause, what it is made of (for instance, 'the ball bounced because it is made of rubber'); or,

   b) its formal cause, how it is structured (for example, 'the ball rolled down the incline because it is spherical'); or,

   c) its efficient cause, what brings it about (e.g., 'the ball rolled across the floor because it was pushed'); or lastly,

   d) its final cause, its purpose; ultimately, we must explain the existence and nature of the ball in terms of its use.

Traditionally, people considered the final cause as the most basic of the four. Things should be explained with purposes. Many Medieval thinkers tried to explain natural events, like the falling of stones, the motion of planets with divine purposes. Viewed in this way, nature becomes the handiwork of God. Descartes rejected the four causes, arguing that final causes cannot be used in the study of matter. Descartes helped to replace explanation by purposes with explanation by physical causal laws.

Descartes also rejected explanation by formal causes, insofar as these required the Aristotelian principles of matter, form and privation. According to this principle all change is the gaining and losing of forms. The form of a thing is its actuality; its matter is its potentiality; and privation is what it is not. So, for example, when water changes from cold to hot, it gains the form of heat. Substantial form contrasts with accidental form. Some forms a thing cannot lose without ceasing to be. Such forms constitute its essence. The substantial form added to matter constitutes the coming to be of a new thing. For example, the substantial form of a human is to be a rational animal. The creation of new person happens when that substantial form mixes with matter. Descartes objected that such formal causes do not explain anything. To try to explain why water heats up by saying that it gains the form of heat is to give no explanation at all.

Medieval tradition had conceived of the universe as a hierarchical organic whole, with different levels of being. Between these levels of being, between the macrocosmic universe and the microcosm man, there existed affinities or correspondences. Accordingly, the universe and natural events could be understood as analogous to the human body or a living organism. This is why the universe contains special secret signs. For example, Paracelus writes: "The Siegewurz root is wrapped in envelope like armor; and this is the magic sign showing that like armor it gives protection against weapons."[3]

Contrast this with Descartes' attempts to quantify nature. According to Descartes, the study of nature should concern itself exclusively with the measurable properties of the world, like size, shape and motion. This puts all natural things on the same level, subject to the same physical laws. It means that things differ only in quantitative ways.

This idea of quantifying implies rejecting as basic the traditional four elements: earth, water, air and fire. Aristotle says that the four elements are characterized by two pairs of contraries: hot and cold and wet and dry. According to Descartes, there is only one kind of matter and all its properties are modifications of extension. Descartes rejects traditional explanations employing the properties of the four elements. He says:

> Compare all their real qualities, their substantial forms, their elements and all their other countless hypotheses with my single hypothesis that all bodies are composed of parts...All that I add to this is that the parts...are of one shape rather than another (AT II 200).

We have seen that he rejects four types of explanation common at the time: purposes, forms, affinities and the four elements. He replaces them with mechanical or causal explanation. We can best understand the conflict between the traditional Medieval and the modern scientific view of the universe in terms of the differing explanations they give.

Some Qualifications

Around 1600, the spirit of the age began to change. Observation and reason undermined the appeal to authorities. Science offered a new kind of explanation of natural events. Descartes embodied the optimism of the new age. By understanding nature, humankind will be able to improve its lot. By understanding ourselves, we will become more free.

Descartes also embodied the questions of this age of transformation. Few scientific thinkers of the time were willing to argue for a wholesale rejection of religious thought, despite the rejection of scholasticism. How could the new science be reconciled with religion? Because the two world views clashed, thinkers needed to go back to basics. The changes gave birth to what is now called epistemology, the philosophical study of knowledge itself. With so much in question, it became important to uncover the foundations of knowledge. Self-conscious reflection upon the sources and standards of knowledge was one of the hall-marks of the modern period. This was mostly due to Descartes. He wrote:

> No more useful inquiry can be proposed than that which seeks to determine the nature and scope of human knowledge (AT X 397).

This is why Descartes was in so many ways a focus for the changes of the time. He saw the need to evaluate methodically and systematically all claims to knowledge, to think about how knowledge is possible, and to reconcile the conflict between the new science and the old religion.

These changes occurred gradually, in fits and starts. Also, despite the radical break with the past, the science of Descartes' time was not like that of today. There was no distinction between the sciences and philosophy. The word `science' retained its original meaning: knowledge. The study of nature was usually called `natural philosophy.' What we today call the scientific model and method was very much a work in progress. Even though Descartes was one of the main pioneers of this transition from scholasticism to the method of today's science, his own thinking still contains many Medieval elements.

2

A Life Well Hidden

Descartes was a private, almost secretive and solitary person, who took as his motto `he lives well who is well hidden.' To keep himself well hidden, Descartes moved house many times during his adult life in Holland. In 1629 he wrote words that epitomize his life: "I have resolved to be hidden behind the canvas in order to hear what people are going to say about it." (AT I 70) Around the important year of 1619-20, Descartes wrote in his private notebook:

> Actors, taught not to let any embarrassment show on their faces, put on a mask. I will do the same. So far, I have been a spectator in this theater which is the world, but I am now about to mount the stage and I come forward masked. (AT X 213)

However, in his later life he became embroiled in controversy. Of course, Descartes had controversial views, but he had attracted vocal pupils who were less diplomatic than himself. Also, though Catholic, he chose to live in Protestant Holland and Sweden. Yet, on this score, Descartes' life was a success. He managed to avoid major quarrels with the Catholic church during his lifetime, even though his views were more controversial than those of the condemned Galileo. The Church placed Descartes' writings on the black list of prohibited books in 1663, by which time his physics was accepted throughout much of Europe.

A Life Well Hidden

Descartes wanted his physics or natural philosophy to be accepted without incurring the wrath of the Church.

The first day of his life was nearly the last (31 March 1596). Descartes inherited from his mother tuberculosis. The new baby coughed so much that the doctor gave him no hope of life. His mother died fourteen months after his birth. René's father was a councilor in the local parliament, and he moved to Rennes where he remarried in 1600. Descartes was brought up by his maternal grandmother. After she died in 1610, Descartes had very little contact with his family, except his sister Jeanne. At the age of ten, in 1606, he started boarding at the traditional Jesuit College de la Flèche, a prestigious school enthusiastically patronized by Henry IV. Life in the school was governed by many rules, and boarders hardly ever even went outside the school.

Descartes left La Flèche in 1614. He may have spent a year in St.-Germain-en-Lay, outside Paris, living alone. It is worth noting that the local Royal Gardens contained caves and fountains with hydraulically powered moving statues, which may be an inspiration for the devices which Descartes describes in his *Treatise on Man*.[1]

Descartes went to the University of Poitiers in 1615 to study law. We have a brief glimpse of his character from the dedication of his thesis. According to this, he "thirsted for the broader rivers of eloquence most ardently. But as they make one crave more knowledge rather than quench one's thirst, they could not satisfy me in the least."[2] It seems that Descartes was undecided about his career. Without entirely giving up the idea of the legal profession, in 1618 he joined the army in the Netherlands, as a gentleman soldier. According to his own account, Descartes was idle and unhappy "in the midst of turmoil and uneducated soldiers."

When he was stationed in Breda, he meet Isaac Beeckman on the 10th November 1618. Beeckman was to change Descartes' life. They met by chance when looking at a mathematical problem on a notice board. Descartes asked Beeckman to translate the Flemish and they soon discovered their mutual interest in mathematics. In his diary the next day, Beeckman wrote: "physico-mathematicians are very rare." Neither had meet anyone else who combined the study of physics and mathematics in so exact a way. Beckman was working in corpuscular physics and he became a mentor for Descartes. Later (23rd March 1619) Descartes wrote to him:

11

You are indeed the one person who has shaken me out of my
nonchalance...When my mind strayed far from serious
concerns, it was you who guided me back down the correct
path.

Between November 1618 and January 1619 they collaborated on
projects concerning falling bodies and hydrostatics, with Beeckman
presenting a problem and guidance and Descartes providing the
solution. In January 1619 Descartes dedicated his manuscript
Compendium Musicae to Beeckman. This is a mathematical treatment
of musical intervals as mathematical ratios, perhaps most notable for
displaying the quality of making magnitudes apparent at a glance.

In March 1619, Descartes traveled to Germany to join the army of
Maximillian in Bavaria. He corresponded frequently with Beeckman,
and on the 26th March 1619, he writes that, after six days intensive
work, he has made four important mathematical discoveries.

During the winter of 1619 Descartes was stationed in Ulm. On the
10th November 1619 Descartes had a series of visions or dreams,
which helped define his life work and which we will describe in detail
in the next chapter. This event marks the beginning of Descartes' work
as a public thinker. He notes that on this day he had discovered `the
fundamental principles of a wonderful discovery' (AT x 373). Before
November 1619, Descartes was primarily interested in mathematics and
was toying with the idea of a universal mathematical method.
Afterwards, his thinking was dedicated to discovering a problem
solving method for all the sciences. More on this in the next chapter.

For the sake of convenience and the risk of artificiality, the rest of
his life may be divided into five periods.

1) Travels and Paris 1619-29

After his vision or dreams, during the year 1620, Descartes started
working more seriously on *The Rules for the Direction of the Mind*.
During the early 1620s Descartes traveled a lot, in Germany, Holland,
Italy and France. Eventually, in mid 1625, he settled in Paris until the
winter of 1628-29, living the sociable life of a gentleman. This stay in
Paris was important because Descartes came to know any other
progressive thinkers and become friends with Mersenne and Mydorge,
both mathematicians and ex-pupils of La Flèche. It is probably around
this time that Descartes became interested in optics and discovered the
law of refraction. Around 1627 Descartes returned to his work on the

Rules, partly because of a renewed interest in physical mechanism due to the influence of his friend Mersenne. But by now, Descartes' interest in mathematics was waning; he visited his old friend Beeckman in October 1628 and told him that he had `nothing more to discover in arithmetic and geometry.' He abandoned his work on the Rules to start a new, more ambitious project.

2) *Holland: the early period 1629-37*

In early 1629 Descartes moved to Holland, where he is said to have liked the climate and comparative quiet and seclusion. It was difficult to have uninterrupted time in Paris. Apparently, in Paris he had some fame and many visitors. Ten years had passed since his dreams, and he had not fulfilled the promise to himself of developing his method for science and philosophy. After beginning a couple of other smaller projects, in April 1630 Descartes wrote to Mersenne:

> You may find strange that I have not persevered with the treatises I began while in Paris. The reason is that ... I was forced to start upon a new project, more extensive than the first. (AT I 137)

This work was to become Descartes' classic *The World*, a broad and pioneering work in physics. Although Descartes had a number of friends in the Netherlands, he also kept his address secret from many, including Mydorge. This was a busy period for him. He conducted philosophical discussions by letter, devoting one day per week to correspondence. He experimented in optics and physiology, and read little. When asked about his library, Descartes is said to have gestured to a carcass he had purchased for dissection. Accompanying *The World* was a treatise on anatomy and physiology called *Man*. Shortly before it was due to be published in 1633, however, he heard of Galileo's condemnation by the Inquisition, and cautiously suppressed his own work for fear of being similarly censured by the Church.

This marks a turning point in Descartes' life. Although his vision had always included metaphysics, in the period after Galileo's condemnation, Descartes' sees more and more the need to give a metaphysical basis for his natural philosophy. Descartes now had two major works unfinished and unpublished. In order to present his physics to the public, he started to work on an essay on meteorology. He also decided to rework some already existing material on optics into a short treatise. In 1635, his friend Reneri started to teach Descartes' natural philosophy at the University of Utrecht. Probably this fact propelled Descartes to finish his revision of the earlier material with more urgency. In the spring of 1636, Descartes decided to put together an essay on algebra and geometry, possibly for the fear that Fermat would publish before him. Meanwhile in the winter of 1635-36, Descartes decided to publish an introductory essay to accompany his more technical works. The full title of this essay is called the `Discourse on the Method of rightly conducting one's reason and seeking the truth in the sciences.' The Discourse is written as autobiographical essay. Descartes choose that medium partly so that others might `imitate what they think worthwhile.' Partly too, Descartes wanted his work to be accessible; for that reason he wrote it in French, instead of the usual Latin.

On the 15th October 1634, Descartes was engaging in another French activity. During this period he was lodging in the house of Thomas Sargeant, who taught in the French school in Amsterdam. On the aforementioned Sunday night, Descartes made love with the maid, Hélène. Their daughter Francine was born on July 19th 1635.

3) Holland: the happy period 1637-1640

When the Discourse was published, Descartes moved to the Dutch coast near Haarlem in August 1637 where he remained until the end of 1639, with Hélène and his daughter Francine, whom he passed off as his niece. Perhaps this was the happiest period of his life. Descartes shows concern for his own looks and mortality. At first, he spend a lot of time dealing with correspondence, mostly objections to the Discourse. He also cultivated a herb garden, dissected animals and gave accounts of the workings and physics of various simple machines such as the pulley, the lever, the cog wheel.

Sometime in 1638 Descartes started work on *the Meditations on First Philosophy*, his main work, about which he wrote to his close friend Mersenne on the 28th January 1641:

> "I may tell you, between ourselves, that these six meditations
> contain the entire foundation for my physics. But it is not
> necessary to say so, if you please, because that might make it
> harder for those who favor Aristotle to approve them. I hope
> that those who read them will gradually accustom themselves

14

to my principles and recognize the truth in them before they
notice that they destroy those of Aristotle." (AT III 297)

The Meditations give the metaphysical and epistemological
foundation of Descartes' physics. Descartes clearly was hoping for
Church approval of his work. First, we can see this in the full title and
the preface containing a dedication to the Theology faculty of the
Sorbonne. The full title of the work is `Meditations on First Philosophy
in which are demonstrated the existence of God and the distinction
between the human soul and the body.' Second, Descartes physics
implies that the Earth is not the still center of the solar system, but he
avoids explicitly stating this. Descartes had the innovative idea of
publishing his work with objections written by leading thinkers of the
time and with Descartes' replies. The 1642 second edition had seven
sets of objections and replies.

Descartes' period of personal happiness ended suddenly in
September 1640, when Francine died of fever. Descartes said that her
death was "the greatest sorrow that he had even experienced in his life."

4) Holland: the mature period: 1640-44

After his daughter's death, a new stage of Descartes' life begins.
We hear no more about Hélène. He moves to a castle near Leiden, and
begins to enjoy a slightly less frugal life than before. During this
period, Descartes enters into an unwelcome religious dispute with
Voetius, a professor of theology at Utrecht. Descartes was obviously
concerned that his work be accepted. Probably to help gain credibility,
he published objections and replies to the Meditations. However to
avoid problems the work was published in Latin. But Descartes'
follower Regius was less cautious than Descartes and put forward some
Cartesian propositions for public discussion in June 1640. Descartes
tried to show that his philosophy was compatible with orthodoxy, but
embroiled himself in a dispute with Voetius, a professor of theology at
the University of Utrecht. As a result, Descartes ended up in an Utrecht
court in June 1643 for slandering a clergyman. The charge was proved
false, but Descartes' life in Netherlands was becoming very difficult.

This acrimonious dispute must have drained Descartes' energies.
His *Epistola ad Voetium* of May 1643 (an open letter giving an
account of the dispute with Voetius and Descartes' defense) was 200
pages in length. This must have interrupted the work which Descartes
had begun in 1641, the *Principles of Philosophy*. Also, it is probably

during this time that Descartes wrote the unfinished dialogue, *The Search for Truth*, only part of which survives. Despite these interruptions, the Principles was ready for the publishers by 1644. The work is divided into four parts and is supposed to be a complete statement of Descartes' natural philosophy and his metaphysics, put in the form of a textbook to rival the standard texts of the time. Remember that Descartes' main work on physics, The World, was not published in his life-time. Despite the comprehensive nature of the Principles, parts five and six of the work, which were supposed to be about living beings and man, were never finished.

During this period Descartes begun his relationship with the Princess Elizabeth of Bohemia. Her family were exiled to the Netherlands in 1620 when she was two. They were not rich and all attempts to find a politically suitable marriage match for Elizabeth failed. She remained single all her life. She was an intellectually strong and active person and continued a relationship, mostly by correspondence, with Descartes from around May 1643. Descartes may well have fallen in love with the young princess, who regarded him as her spiritual and intellectual mentor. His letters to her are sometimes surprisingly intimate. In any case, she changed his life.

4) Later days: 1644 -1650

Around the middle of 1645 Descartes' correspondence with Elizabeth resumes in earnest after a break, and as a result, his interest in the passions becomes deeper. Elizabeth stimulates Descartes to think more about the practical implications of his views of the mind -body relation. He becomes more interested in the effect of the mind on the body and less in the effect of the body on the mind. In other words, his thinking about feelings becomes less physiological and more humanist. His book *The Passions* was probably written between 1645-6.

In August 1646 Descartes visited Elizabeth for the last time. Her family moved from the Netherlands, after her brother killed a French officer. Her move may have unsettled Descartes. On May 10 1647 he traveled to France and he wrote to Elizabeth:

> The letter I have received from your highness leads me to
> hope that you will return to The Hague towards the end of the
> summer. Indeed, I may tell you that this is the chief reason
> why I would prefer to live in this country rather than any
> other. .. A troop of theologians, followers of the scholastic

philosophy, seem to have formed a league in an attempt to crush me by their slanders.

As Descartes' controversy with Voetius finished, a new dispute began at the University of Leiden. A follower of Descartes had begun to teach a version of his philosopher and this attracted the critical attention of the professors of Theology who brought various charges against Descartes.

During this period Descartes' regained his interest in anatomy. He was dissecting and he wrote a short treatise, *A Description of the Human Body*. In 1648 Descartes published his *Notes against a Program*. Earlier, in 1645 Regius, Descartes' follower, had sent him a copy of his own book on physics. Descartes thought that the book contained profound errors. Against Descartes' advice, Regius published the book in 1646 and the following year Descartes writes in the preface to the French edition of the Principles: " I am obliged to disavow his work entirely." The *Notes Against a Program* was dedicated to showing the mistakes of Regius's approach, i.e. of doing natural philosophy without a proper metaphysical basis. This same year, in April 1648, Franz Burman, a 20 year old student dined with Descartes and interviewed him. The record of this interview was unknown and unpublished for 250 years, but since has become part of the philosophical legacy of Descartes.

Around this time, it became clear to Descartes that Elizabeth would not return to the Netherlands. He began to think of moving to France. He visited Paris again in May 1648. But the city was in the middle of a revolt and Descartes left. He decided to move to Sweden. In 1645, Chanut, who was a friend and admirer of Descartes, moved to Sweden to work as the French liaison officer, and later ambassador, in the court of the young intellectual Queen Christina. Chanut mediated a relation between the Queen and Descartes, and by 1646 Descartes was feeling that the persecution in Netherlands against him was bad enough to consider the patronage of the Queen and a move to Sweden. Perhaps Descartes thought that he would receive the honors due to him in Sweden. At first Descartes hesitated. Finally, he agreed to accept the invitation and Christina sent a battleship and an admiral to receive him. On the 1st October 1649 Descartes arrived in Sweden. The Queen planned for Descartes to become a Swedish noble of her court. At first his tasks were minimal. He had to set his unpublished papers into order and form an academy for Swedish scholars. However, in January 1650, he began to give the Queen five hour long philosophy lessons three times a week at 5. a.m. For years Descartes had been in the habit of spending mornings reading and writing in bed. Now his coach took him to the palace at 4.30 in the morning. Moreover, the winter was exceptionally harsh. Chanut caught pneumonia and Descartes helped to nurse him. However, Descartes himself contracted the disease on February 1st. He died on 11 February 1650. Even after death Descartes was surrounded in controversy, because Queen Christina converted to Catholicism in 1652. Descartes and Chanut were accused by the Swedish Lutherans of trying to convert her.

Here is the list of Descartes' main works. 1629: Rules for the Direction of the Mind. 1634: The World. 1637: Discourse on the Method . 1641: Meditations Concerning First Philosophy (including six Objections and Replies). 1644: Principles of Philosophy. 1647: Notes against a Certain program. 1648: A Description of the Human Body. 1649: The Passions of the Soul. To this list, we should add the unfinished dialogue, The Search for Truth, which was published posthumously. There is also Burman's notes of his discussion with Descartes in 1648, called The Conversation. Of course, we should also add Descartes' many letters on philosophical issues, which he wrote throughout his life.

Looking over Descartes' life, tentatively we can identify four important phases in his intellectual development. As a young man he was mostly interested in what we might call today applied mathematics; he had a practical or problem solving approach to mathematics. Even as a very young man, he had the idea that his new approach to mathematics could be applied to other areas of knowledge and that the sciences should be unified. He started to work seriously in the sciences or natural philosophy around 1629, which is the beginning of the second phase of his life, during which he worked on *The World*. The condemnation of Galileo in 1633 probably initiates the next, the third phase, in which Descartes becomes much more actively interested in articulating the metaphysical basis of his natural philosophy. During this period he writes the *Discourse*, the *Meditations* and finally the *Principles*. Around 1644 Descartes enters into the final, fourth phase of his intellectual life in which he becomes more concerned with the application of his philosophy to human life and ethics. Even though there are important changes in emphasis in his thinking and important differences of detail, it is remarkable to what extent the body of Descartes' work is one consistent whole. We can find traces of his latest work on the passions in his earliest notebooks. It is as if the whole flower is contained in the seeds.

3

Rules For a Method

On the cold night of November 10, 1619, near Ulm in Bavaria, Descartes had three dreams. His dreams apparently revealed his life's mission. To escape the cold, he had shut himself in a stove or a small stove heated room. During the day he had meditated deeply and began to doubt his beliefs. Hours of intense effort brought him to a revelation of the unity of the sciences, of all knowledge. He felt that he had in his grasp a marvelous new science to replace current confusions.

The same night he had the three consecutive dreams which he felt were divine indications of his vocation. First he saw himself staggering around in a kind of whirlwind which seemed to affect no–one else. He awoke, prayed for protection and meditated on good and evil for almost two hours before sleeping again. A piercing noise startled him awake the second time, and he saw his room full of sparks. This apparently had happened to him on other occasions; so after blinking several times he was able to fall asleep again. The third dream was more complicated and involved several books, the words "Quod vitae sectabor iter" and a stranger who gave him some verses beginning "Est et non". One of the books had been a kind of encyclopedia, which Descartes felt represented the sciences gathered together. "Quod vitae sectabor iter" was the counsel of a wise man or moral theology, while the poem "Est et Non", the Yes and No of Pythagorus, stood for truth and error. Descartes understood these dreams to be a revelation that his life's work was to unite all knowledge according to geometrical

19

principles.

These dreams help us understand Descartes' motivation as a philosopher. His vision is to find a method which will enable him to explain all natural phenomena in terms of a few basic principles. However, according to Descartes, this scientific vision was divinely given to him. From his point of view, the content of the vision cannot be in conflict with its source, and therefore, his future work in science should be compatible with the basic doctrines of the Church. In gratitude for his vision, Descartes made a pilgrimage to the shrine of the Virgin of Loretto probably in the year 1624.

After his experience, Descartes began to seek the method which would unveil the secrets of the universe and reveal the unity of the sciences. But his early work was sporadic and it concentrated primarily on mathematics. In May 1622 Descartes sold various properties given to him by his father. He was free to do as he wished. In effect, he spent the next four years traveling, until he settled in Paris in 1626. In the *Discourse* where he reports on these experiences, Descartes writes that to develop his method, he would have to discover certainties in philosophy, and that he needed more preparation and maturity to do that.

The preparation lasted until the fall of 1628 when Descartes was invited to reply to a talk given by the chemist Chandoux in Paris. The talk, criticizing scholastic philosophy, was well received, but Descartes' reply was even better received. Descartes argued that philosophy needed a new method for arriving at certainty. Impressed by this performance, cardinal Pierre Bérulle convinced Descartes to quit Paris social life, and dedicate himself to working on his new method.

His first book is the *Rules for the Direction of the Mind*, which Descartes had started writing in 1620. He also worked on the book in 1627-9, but finally abandoned it, as his interests shifted away from mathematics and method towards physics. In September 1629 Descartes moved to Holland, where he could work without interruption. Shortly afterwards, he started writing his masterpiece, *The World*, a unified explanation of all natural phenomena, which he withdrew. Descartes' first published work was the *Discourse on the Method* (1637). The work basically consists on three essays with a long introduction on method. The three essays, which use material from his unfinished book *The World*, concern Optics, Meteorology and Geometry. The Introduction aims to outline the new method for arriving at truth and the three essays aim to illustrate the method in practice. Each essay in itself is an important work.

Reading these early books, one is struck by three features of Descartes' vision. First, he tries to contain all knowledge into one unified system or science, which is based on a few simple principles. The breadth of this enterprise is astonishing. His work *The World* contains chapters on heat, light, weight, the formation of the planets, the nature of comets, the formation of the earth, the tides, the laws of nature, and a treatise on physiology. In seeking the unifying principles behind all of these natural phenomena, Descartes aims to make the workings of nature clear. Understanding nature is no longer a question of interpreting God's mind, finding occult clues to solve mysteries, but instead it is a question of discovering the basic mechanisms which govern matter. In an early notebook probably written between 1619 and 1622, he wrote:

> The sciences are present masked, but if the masks were taken off, they would be revealed in all their beauty. If we could see how the sciences are linked together, we would find them no harder to grasp than the series of numbers. (ATX 315)

Second, to achieve this, Descartes must demonstrate those principles, and defend them. This requires a method for gaining knowledge. The new science needs an epistemology which in turn needs a metaphysics. To unify, science must be methodical but to find a method, Descartes must consciously reflect on the nature of knowledge.

Third, given its historical context, one is impressed by the freshness of Descartes' whole project. Despite the fact that modern science has other important advocates and pioneers, like Galileo and Francis Bacon, Descartes' work embarks on an adventure into new territories of knowledge. Furthermore, compared to the Latin textbooks of the time, Descartes' books are written in an engaging and personal style. He often mixes autobiography with philosophy. Moreover, the *Discourse* and *The World* were written in French. Academic books of the time were usually written in Latin.

The Rules

Let us concentrate of the first work: *Rules for the Direction of the Mind.* It contains 21 rules for the direction of the mind (the complete version was supposed to contain 36). The aim of the book is to provide a method to guide the mind so that it can pass true and solid judgments on whatever it is investigating. (Rule 1). Explaining this aim of his study, Descartes stresses the unity of the sciences, "for they are all interconnected and interdependent." (ATX 361). Descartes concludes that we need a general method, which at the same time helps people to increase their powers of reasoning.

Descartes developed his basic idea by consciously reflecting on why certainty is achievable in mathematics. According to Descartes, knowledge requires certainty. In the second rule, he says that we should resolve only to believe what we can be certain of. In particular, Descartes rejects the merely probable syllogisms of the scholastic philosophers, and chastises them for concentrating on constructing "subtle conjectures" regarding difficult problems. Instead we should take the simple problems of arithmetic and geometry as our model. Why are the results of these two branches of knowledge certain? As Descartes says in rule four, "we need a method..." (ATX 371).

Later, writing in the *Discourse* about the earlier period of his life, Descartes claims that he had success applying his method: "by strictly observing the few rules I had chosen, I became very adept at unraveling all the questions" of geometry and arithmetic. The task he set himself was to develop from this method a general approach for all problem solving and investigation. Most investigators study haphazardly without method. Method means certain and easy to follow rules, which avoid error and if used in the right order and way will lead to as complete a knowledge as possible.

a) The Basis

According to Descartes, the essence of the mathematical method is to start with propositions which can be intuited as clearly and obviously true, and to deduce from them results in a step by step manner. The two key ingredients are self- evident intuitions and step by step deduction. First, we need to be able to start with truths that are self-evident to intuition. In mathematics such truths can be found because the data of mathematics is entirely simple, precise and abstract. Intuition is the capacity to mentally grasp or see the truth of such simple propositions. Descartes gives the following examples: I can intuit that I exist, and that a triangle has three sides. These are truths which are known by the light of reason. By concentrating on clear examples of such truths, rather than on more complex difficult issues, we can develop our powers of intuition. Intuition is the direct intellectual perceiving of a simple truth and therefore it is free from doubt.

Second, we need to be able to deduce the logical implications of the simple truths we can intuit. Deduction is the capacity to move from one simple to another, when the first implies the second. According to Descartes, deduction has much in common with intuition. Descartes conceives reasoning or deduction as a chain of links between propositions. In deductive reasoning the links can be seen with the same certainty of insight as with intuition. Deduction is like intuition on the move. intuition is all at once and deduction is successive.

The fact that all reasoning has intuition as its base has three important implications for Descartes. First, to preserve certainty in our deductions, we need to go step by step, in such a way that all the steps are self-evident. Second, given that we do this, deduction will be infallible. This is because reasoning just consists in following the logical implications of simple and clear ideas. Intuition reveals the first step in the chain, and provided we proceed with care, each step will be as certain as the previous one. Thirdly, given that all discursive reasoning has intuition as its base, we can hope that the method can be applied to any area of knowledge.

This is the basis of Descartes method. We can see why it applies to mathematics par excellence. Mathematics consists solely in deducing logical consequences from simple, self-evident data. It fits perfectly Descartes' picture of the powers of the knowing mind: intuition and deduction.

b) The General Method

Rules five, six and seven state the general principles of Descartes' method. (These three rules plus the second are repeated in the *Discourse*). Five says that we should reduce complex propositions into simpler ones, until we arrive at the simplest ones of all. From these we can rebuild knowledge from the simples. The idea is that propositions can be ordered according to what is known on the basis of what (or epistemological priority). Descartes himself notes that this is a significant departure from the scholastic tradition, according to which things are classified into categories or some ontological scheme. Descartes' idea is more practical because it leads us back to basics. Rule six is supposed to make this idea more concrete by explaining what counts as `simple.' Rule seven gives us a way to "ascend" from the simplest propositions, back to those which depend on them.

Descartes gives us an example of this in Rule 8, a problem of refraction.

Q1 What is the shape of a lens that focuses parallel rays of light on to the same point?

Q2 What is the relation between the angle of incidence and the angle of refraction?

Q3 How is refraction caused by light passing from one medium to another?

Q4 How does a ray of light penetrate a transparent body?

Q5 What is light?

Q6 What is a natural power?

We start with the first question, but we see that to answer that, we need to answer 2 and so on, until we arrive at question 6 which is a simple question, answerable by intuition. From that answer we can deduce the answer to question 5 and so on until we answer our original question.[1]

c) *The Important Specifics*

The really important aspect of the method emerges from Descartes' detailed discussion. Descartes thinks that he has a method for solving any mathematical problem concerning numbers and figures. Given this, he wants to show how to reformulate any scientific problem in terms of numbers and figures, such as points and lines. Later in life Descartes explicitly argues that all facts about the material world can be expressed in geometric terms. Given this, both the method and unity of the sciences should follow. This was a part of his early vision.

What do Descartes' mathematical innovations consist in? Basically in three points. First he invented the symbolism which enables us to represent equations algebraically in this form $y = a + bx$ (using `x', 'y' and 'z' for unknown variables and 'a', 'b' and 'c' for constants). He also invented the standard symbolism for squares, cubes and higher powers, $x \div x$ etc. This is important because it indicates a level of abstractedness not reached before. Second, this enabled him to see the unity of geometry and algebra. He developed the idea of graphs with coordinates and axis, so that an equation like $X = 3 + 2y$ could be represented as a specific line, others as curves. In this way addition and subtraction, multiplication and division could all be represented geometrically by figures. E.g. if a and b represent lines then a x b is represented by the rectangle bounded by those lines. Thirdly, all this enabled him to solve equations with two unknown variables, something which had not been done before.

Reviewing Descartes' whole method, we see, first, that it is clearly non-authoritarian. It liberates the individual to seek for himself or herself. It this way, it carries the spirit of a new age and is powerful politically. Second, it is fundamentally non-empiricist. Descartes does not ignore sense perception, as we shall see. Although he argues that it is a confused, distorted and uncertain form of knowledge, it has an important place in science, once its subordinate relation to reason is understood. However, Descartes thinks of his method not only as rule-tool for investigation, but also as a training for the mind, to help liberate it from prejudice and the influence of the senses. Third, being mathematical, the method allows for precision and mechanical explanations within the sciences. It permits explanations of material change in terms of what we now call the laws of physics. Lastly, Descartes' method is psychological. It is not formal in the way that Aristotle's theory of the syllogism is. Descartes is more interested in how the mind must function in a search for truth.

This last point gives Descartes a problem. He thinks of intuition as an innate capacity. He calls it the light of reason and assumes that it is reliable. He assumes that the intellect cannot make mistakes, once it is used properly. But how can he be sure of this? To answer this question requires work in philosophy and metaphysics, which Descartes felt that he was not ready to do in 1619. But his own method seems to require it. The method itself needs a metaphysical justification.

4

The World

The World was supposed to be published in 1633. Descartes withdrew it after the condemnation of Galileo. The work divides into four parts: the first, chapters 1-6, explains Descartes' theory of matter; the second, consisting of chapters six to twelve, concerns cosmology; the third is Descartes' theory of light; and the fourth is the physiological treatise, *Man*. What was originally conceived as a treatise on light became a book about the whole universe, because (as Descartes explains to Mersenne), `all these problems in physics are so interlinked and depend so much on one another.' (AT I 140) In this chapter we shall explain Descartes' natural philosophy, saving the philosophical underpinnings of his physics for Ch. 8, once we are more familiar with his metaphysics.

1) Matter in Motion

The idea of matter in motion is sufficient to explain all natural phenomena. According to Descartes, matter is spatial extension; all the properties of matter are merely different ways of being extended. This means that Descartes thinks that all natural changes can be explained by the spatial properties of matter in motion. Descartes replaces the traditional idea of the four elements with that of different sizes of corpuscles of matter.

In chapter one, Descartes argues that our perceptual ideas of the world do not resemble their causes (see Ch. 5). Descartes needs this claim to make his physics plausible, since the world as described by his physics is quite different from the world as perceived by us.

He begins with the example of fire. Fire burns by setting the minute particles of the wood in motion, separating them into fire, air, smoke and ash. Descartes contrasts this kind of explanation which requires only the idea of matter in motion with the traditional scholastic one in terms of forms and qualities. He writes: " Let others imagine in this wood, if they like, the form of fire, the quality of heat....I am content to conceive here only the movement of parts" (AT XI 7). Descartes explains the difference between solids and fluids in similar terms. If they are at rest with regard to each other, the minute parts of a body will not separate, unless a force is applied to them. In solids, the corpuscles are stationary with respect to each other. In fluids they are in motion. And in gases, more so. Fire is the most active form of matter. In other words, Descartes explains the different properties of matter in terms of the rate of relative motion of the parts.

According to Descartes, all things are in motion. The quantity of motion in the universe is always conserved. Descartes realizes that such a conservation principle is required for mathematical mechanics. His basic claim that matter is extension rules out the possibility of a vacuum. To answer the question `how can bodies move when there is no empty space to move into?', Descartes gives the example of fish swimming in a pool. The water is displaced, even when there is no sign of it on the surface. Descartes uses this to illustrate his idea that all motion is circular. As the fish swims, the water in front of it is displaced from, and the water behind it flows into the space it previously occupied. This is a circular movement of water. This is a nice way to picture Descartes' view of all movement in the universe.

Descartes thinks that there three sizes of particle. This is best understood in terms of light. Light is generated by fire, which consists in the very fine type of particle. Light is transmitted through a celestial medium, which consists of the second type of particle. Light is reflected and refracted by the third and grossest type of particle.

b) Cosmology

To avoid actually affirming the heretical claim that the Earth is in motion around the Sun, Descartes constructs a hypothetical universe, based solely on the principles of his physics. Later, he will argue that this hypothetical universe is indistinguishable from the actual universe.

In this universe, matter is the same as extension, and therefore the whole of space is full of one single body, the parts of which move at different rates. In such a universe the particles are in constant collision, and their motion is determined by three laws. Descartes sharply distinguishes the power and the direction of movement. The first law asserts that a body will conserve its motion unless in collision with another; the second that the total amount of motion of bodies in collision is constant. The third law affirms that bodies will move in a straight line in the absence of external factors (in reality things move in a circle because of the factors explained in the fish example above).

Descartes conceives of a universe in which all matter is in motion swirling around as if in an indefinite number of whirlpools or vortices. Descartes employs this idea to explain the formation and movement of the sun and stars (ch.8). Planets move around the sun by being carried in the celestial fluid, like a boat in a stream. On this basis, Descartes tries to explain why some planets have a faster orbit than others (ch. 9), and why the moon orbits the Earth (ch.10). Descartes employs the same theory to explain the complex variations in the movement of the tides (ch. 12). These tidal cycles he explains in terms of circular movement of the celestial matter around the Earth.

c) Light

Writing in the *Discourse* about his unpublished treatise *The World*, Descartes says:

> I undertook to expound fully only what I knew about light.
> Then as the opportunity arose, I added something about the
> Sun and fixed stars, because almost all of it comes from them;
> the heavens because they transmit it; the planets comets and
> Earth because they reflect light; and especially bodies on the
> earth, because they are colored or transparent...; and finally
> about man, because he observes these bodies. (AT VI 42)

According to Descartes, light travels through the air, the second element and is reflected and refracted by things made up of the third kind of particles. All behavior of light is explicable according to the laws of motion. To show this Descartes lists 12 properties of light and shows how his theory can explain them. To explain reflection, he uses the analogy of a tennis ball being reflected off the surface of a canvas. To explain refraction, he uses the example of a ball passing through water. Descartes develops a geometrical model of these physical actions, which includes the sin law of refraction, from which he was able to calculate the refractive index from air to water.

In his later work the *Meteorology*, Descartes uses the theory of refraction to explain rainbows. In the same work, he explains colors in terms of the speed of rotation of the particles of the second element. He tries to explain why rainbows appear as they do at the angles they do.

d) Physiology

To describe the physiology of human beings, Descartes describes the workings of `earthen machines' which would indistinguishable from the human organism. Descartes tries to explain all physiological processes - digestion, the heart, the circulation of the blood and the nervous system. He thinks that all human functions can be explained mechanically, except those requiring free-will and self-consciousness thought. Descartes conceives of the nerves as a system of tiny pipes, along which a fluid-like substance moved changing the shape of the muscles. As well as explaining breathing, sneezing, coughing, and yawning, Descartes tries to account for perceptual mechanisms, including the lenses of the eye and the perception of distance.

From Physics to Metaphysics

After Descartes withdrew *The World*, he rewrote two unpublished essays, The *Dioptrics* and *Meteorology*, and added a third, *Geometry*, to illustrate his method and discoveries. He added an introductory essay *Discourse on the Method* and published all four works as one book in 1637. Probably, this format was to Descartes' taste. He liked writing in sporadic fits. This way he could show off his method, without revealing its implications for planetary motion and risking the censure of the Church. In any case, the *Discourse* was published anonymously.

The condemnation of Galileo shifted Descartes' focus from natural philosophy to metaphysics. The *Discourse* points out the general need for a metaphysical foundation for the method and tries to provide one. However, Descartes was not satisfied with this part of his work. It was completed in a rush. The book was already at the printers and Descartes was still writing! For these reasons, he began work on the *Meditations*, his most known philosophical work.

5

The Challenge of Doubt

The First Meditation is one of the most famous pieces of philosophical writing. In it Descartes raises philosophical doubts concerning the existence of material objects. This compressed piece of philosophy presents us, the reader, with two challenges. The first is to not dismiss out of hand the doubts Descartes raises. Instead, we must understand his arguments and not be satisfied with superficial objections. The second is: how should we reply to his arguments? Later in the Meditations, Descartes himself answers the doubts. However, his way out is questionable and, therefore, we cannot escape the force of the doubts of the First Meditation in the way that Descartes tries to. We inherit his problem, but not his solution.

The ultimate aim of Descartes' Method of Doubt is simply to find certainties, propositions which can serve as a secure foundation in the reconstruction of knowledge. In particular, for Descartes it is the first step in establishing the metaphysical grounding for his physics. This is the way forward. Pushing Descartes from behind is the fact that, before even raising any doubts, he realizes that many of his beliefs are unreliable and based on superstition. However, he cannot be sure which are reliable and which are not. Descartes criticizes scholastic philosophy for providing only probable syllogisms; so, he must offer certainty. The solution is to wipe the slate clean with the Method of Doubt, and use those certainties which survive this cleaning process as the foundation in reconstructing knowledge. Knowledge must be based on certainty and we gain certainty by rejecting the uncertain. In the Synopsis to the Meditations Descartes explains:

> Although the utility of a doubt so general may not at first be apparent, it is nevertheless very great, in that (such doubt) delivers us from all sorts of prejudices, and prepares for us a very easy way of accustoming our mind to detaching itself from the senses and finally, in that it brings it about that it is no longer possible that we can have any doubt about that which we afterwards discover to be true. (AT VII,12)

The Method of Doubt is also a psychological exercise, to help the reader free herself from the influence of the senses. We are accustomed to think that the world is how we perceive it to be. According to Descartes, this is a prejudice. To achieve his aims, Descartes has to make doubt systematic. He cannot call each one of his beliefs into doubt, one by one; so he must undermine their support.

To doubt does not mean thinking that our beliefs are false. It means suspending judgment as to their truth, neither believing nor disbelieving. Believing involves both having an idea in one's mind and also judging that the idea is true. To assent to the idea of p is to believe p; to deny the idea of p is to disbelieve p. When one doubts p, however, one suspends judgment as to the truth or falsity of p. In effect, Descartes Method of Doubt amounts to withholding the judgment that anything in the external world corresponds to or causes the idea in the mind. Ideas are the immediate objects of cognition and the external world is known only mediately through these ideas. The notion of an idea as the immediate object of cognition is latent in Descartes' Method.

The Method of Doubt consists of three stages, each more radical than its predecessor. Descartes does not want to show merely that doubt is logically possible. He argues for the much stronger conclusion that doubt is reasonable. Each of the stages of doubt gives an argument for this conclusion. Earlier we discussed the usefulness of doubt, and this may hide the important point: according to the First Meditation, we do not have adequate evidence to claim that we know what external objects exist. This presents the reader with two challenges.

1) The First Stage

The Challenge of Doubt

First, Descartes notes that many of his beliefs are derived from sense perception. He points out that sense perception has deceived him in the past, especially with minute and distant objects. He claims that it is foolish to trust something which has been known to deceive us. He concludes that we should not trust those beliefs based on the senses. We might represent his argument as follows:

1. Most of my beliefs are based on the senses
2. The senses have deceived me in the past
3. It is reasonable to doubt something which has deceived me
4. Thus, most of my beliefs are open to reasonable doubt.

According to Descartes, this argument does not legitimize a very universal doubt, because many sense derived beliefs seem certain. For example, he thinks that, merely on the basis of this argument, he cannot legitimately doubt that he has a body and that he is now sitting in front of the fire. Such doubts require a more radically inspired argument. Probably what he means is that premise 3 is false. Sometimes sense perception apparently does not deceive us and it would not be rational to condemn the senses wholesale, on the basis of some deceptions.

Notice that Descartes does not argue from the premise that any sense experience could be an illusion to the conclusion that all sense experiences could collectively be an illusion. Such an argument would involve a fallacy because the universal possibility of illusion does not entail the possibility of universal illusion.[1] This argument involves the fallacy of composition. Any person could earn above the average salary does not entail that all could. However, Descartes does not commit this fallacy. Also we should note that Descartes' argument in this first stage of doubt is not the same as the so-called argument from illusion which we will be considering later in the chapter.

2) *The Second Stage*

Next, Descartes asks how he can be certain that he is not dreaming. He recalls the lucid dreams that he has had in the past. For example, he has dreamed that he is awake and sitting by the fire, just as he actually is now. Lucid dreams are indistinguishable from waking experience, and in them one may believe that one is actually awake. So, although usually dreams are often more chaotic than waking experiences, it can be impossible to distinguish between a dream and a waking experience. There are no internal criteria or signs by which one can tell whether one is awake or merely dreaming. Any given situation could be an illusion: it could be a dream. Descartes' argument can be represented by the following syllogism:

1. There are no internal criteria by which one distinguish dreaming from waking sense experience
2. Dream experiences are usually false
3. Thus, any of my waking sense experiences could be false
4. All my beliefs are based on sense experience
5. Therefore, all of my beliefs could be false

Descartes asserts, however, that this argument too is not enough to legitimize a universal doubt. Dreams must be made up of elements from reality, and these simple elements, such as shape, size, number, and time, must be real. When Descartes says this, he is qualifying premise 2. Usually dream experiences are false in the sense that what you are dreaming is not actually happening in reality. However, dream experiences are not completely false, in the sense that they contain elements from reality. Descartes also says that even if he supposes that he is now dreaming, two plus three still equals five and a square only has four sides. When he says this he is reminding us that premise 4 is false. Some truths are known through reason.

Despite Descartes' misgivings about his own argument, some philosophers have questioned the validity of this second stage of doubt. One objection says that, even if it is possible that I am now dreaming, it is not possible that I dream all the time. The possibility of dream experiences requires that some experiences are not dreams. However, this objection does not quite seem to hit the mark. His point is not to claim that we could be dreaming all the time; it is rather that we have no internal evidence or criteria which surely distinguishes dreaming and waking experience. Any particular experience could be a dream.

3) The Third Stage

The first and second stages only take us so far. Only the third and most radical stage succeeds in introducing a universal doubt about the existence of external objects. It consists in the possibility of a malicious spirit. Descartes supposes there could be a supremely powerful and intelligent spirit who does his utmost to deceive him. In which case, Descartes says, he might even be deceived into thinking that two plus three equals five. It seems that the possibility of a malicious demon leaves none of our former beliefs free from legitimate doubt. At this third stage of the Method, doubt is as universal and radical as it can be. Any beliefs immune from this kind of doubt will be certain.

The third stage of doubt introduces a radical scepticism. For if there were a powerful deceiving demon, I would be mistaken in thinking that my sense experiences correspond to and are caused by external objects at all. The possibility of a demon supports the doubt as to whether material objects exist at all. What exactly is the argument of the third Stage of Doubt? We can lay out this argument as follows:

1. There could be an powerful spirit deceiving me
2. If there were such a demon, then I would be mistaken in all my beliefs
_____
3 Therefore my former beliefs could be mistaken

The crucial premise is the first - there could be an powerful, deceiving spirit? It means that we have no evidence to the contrary. We have no evidence against the claim that there is such a demon. We can understand Descartes' argument in contemporary terms by comparing it to the under-determination of theory by data in contemporary science. (However, this comparison is not part of Descartes' actual text). The under-determination of theory by data occurs when we have two hypothesis which explain the empirical data equally well. The empirical data by itself is not sufficient to support one theory over the other. In the case of the third stage of doubt, we have two theories: one is that the empirical data is caused by external physical objects in space and the other is that it is caused by a powerful deceiving spirit. These two theories explain the empirical data itself - the sensory ideas that I am now having - equally well. There is no good reason, as far as the data is concerned, for thinking one of the theories more likely true than the other. This comparison helps to support premise 1 in the above argument.

This helps us to understand another aspect of the three stages of doubt. Progressively they force us to make a sharp distinction between the idea perceived and the external cause of that perception. Descartes brings out this distinction very nicely in the *World*. Imagine a feather tickling your lips. Is there anything actually in the feather which remotely resembles your sensation? No; of course not. Similarly, argues Descartes, what we see does not resemble what is the objects. Seeing is like being tickled by light. Hearing is like being tickled by air waves. Descartes says in the Optics:

Likewise the movements in the nerves leading to the ears
make the soul hear sounds... But in all these there need be no
resemblance between the ideas which the soul conceives and
the movements which cause these ideas. (AT VI 130)

Given this point, the second and third stages of doubt effectively ask us
two questions.

First, can you imagine having an experience exactly like the one
you are having now, except that the duplicate experience is not caused
by external objects at all? The answer seems to have to be: "yes; I can
imagine it." We seem forced to that answer because the cause of
perception lies outside the perception itself.

Second, do you have any evidence that your current experience is
not that duplicate? The answer seems to have to be: "no; I have no such
evidence." We seem forced to that answer because we have already
admitted that the duplicate experience is exactly like the other. So,
there is no possible evidence to distinguish between them.

Two Other Arguments

The argument of the third stage of doubt affirms that there two
equally good possible hypotheses to explain the data of the senses: the
deceiving demon and the existence of material objects.

The weak point in his ingenious argument is the assumption that
the data of experience consist solely in ideas. Descartes' argument
assumes that the data of the senses are ideas in the mind (and not
information concerning external objects). Effectively his argument
presupposes that we perceive our own ideas, and not objects in the
external world. According to Descartes, if you claim "the book I am
now looking at has a white cover" then you have made a mistake, for
you do not perceive the book; you perceive an idea which you presume
to be caused by a book. However, on the other side, against Descartes,
usually when we refer to scientific data, such data already assumes the
perception of objects. Data includes readings from instruments, the
behavior of objects under different conditions. Therefore, is Descartes
entitled to assume that the relevant data of experience consists in ideas?

The answer is that there are positive arguments for Descartes'
view. In the Discourse, he says "even though we see the sun very
clearly we should not judge on that account that it is only as large as we

35

see it." (AT VI 40). Compare this with a story about a four year old boy: `One day John Edgar, who had often seen airplanes take off, rise and gradually disappear into the distance, took his first plane ride. When the plane stopped ascending.....John Edgar turned to his father and said in a rather relieved and puzzled tone of voice, "Things don't really get smaller up here."[2] Descartes would love this example; it fits well with what he says about the prejudices of childhood.

Descartes gives similar arguments in the *World* in order to distinguish what is perceived (the idea itself) from its external cause, and to argue that the first need not resemble the second. This type of argument, based on the thorough-going relativity of perception, stretches back to Plato and beyond, was very influential in Empiricist thought into the twentieth century. The basic thrust of the argument is based on the following principle:

P1. What we perceive can change even when the external object does not, and therefore the two cannot be identical.

To use Descartes' own example from the *Discourse*, when we get jaundice everything looks yellow, but the world itself stays the same. We can summarize the argument as follows:

1. The properties of an external object cannot change without a change occurring in the object itself.
2. What I perceive can change without any change in the object itself.
_____
3. Therefore, what I perceive are not the real properties of an external object.

This may be called the argument from illusion. It has a radical conclusion; it means that we do not perceive things in the world. Given that, it is reasonable to conclude that we perceive only our own ideas.

Implicit in the second and third stages of doubt, there is a principle with a similar thrust to the one above:

P2. What we perceive can remain the same, even if there were no external object at all, and therefore the two cannot be identical.

This principle generates may be called the argument from mirage or hallucination and it can be put as follows.

1. What I perceive can remain the same, even if the external object changes or even disappears
2. If X and Y are the same, then one cannot change without the other changing
3 Therefore, what I perceive is not an external object

Once again, this implies that we do not perceive external objects at all. From this, we seem forced to admit that we can only ever perceive our own ideas, even though this conclusion drags into apparently inescapable scepticism. Given that we can perceive only our own ideas, scepticism follows. At this point, we should be able to appreciate the force of Descartes' challenge to us.

Doubt as a Tool

Despite all this, Descartes is not a sceptic. For him, doubt is only a means.[3] It is not an end in itself. It is a means in both a philosophical and psychological way.

Psychologically, the Meditations are a series of reflections presented in an autobiographical style to encourage others to go through the same process of deliberation. Descartes says: "if the reader cares to follow, he makes it his own as if he had discovered it himself." AT VII 155 Descartes advocates doubting as an art. This art will free us liberate us from the influence of the senses. Descartes wants his readers to be free of the senses, because he thinks that this is a psychological condition of accepting his natural philosophy or physics.

Descartes thinks that we acquire many prejudices during childhood when "the mind was so immersed in the body that it knew nothing distinctly.." (AT IV 114). In the *Principles*, he writes that, as children, we simply assume that things existing outside the mind are similar to sensations, as did the four year old John Edgar mentioned earlier. Unless corrected, this prejudice (namely that the senses giving us knowledge of how the world really is) continues into adulthood. In 1638, Descartes writes: "those who want discover truth must distrust opinions rashly acquired in childhood." (ATII 39) A person attached to the senses could not accept the view of the universe portrayed by Descartes' physics.

Looked at in this way, the Meditations are a set of exercises. The first Meditation offers us a sceptical therapy against the prejudices of childhood. Descartes says: "once in life everything ought to be completely overturned and ought to be rebuilt from the first foundations."[4] Doubt is a strategy and a tool for freeing the mind from the influence of the senses.

The practice of the art of doubt requires the reader to exercise the will in only consenting to clear and distinct ideas or to withhold assent to the confused ideas of the senses. By practicing this art, we will become used to assenting only to clear and distinct ideas, and this is the simple essence of Descartes' whole method. According to Descartes, sceptical therapy is psychologically necessary for the thinker to turn away from the senses and discover the basis of natural science.

Doubt is also a philosophically necessary tool. Remember that Descartes' ultimate aim in the Meditations is to give his physics a metaphysical foundation. The way of clear and distinct ideas, which is the antidote to scepticism, will imply a quantifiable, mechanistic and unified view of science, as we shall see later.

For all these reasons, Descartes' ultimate quarry and concern in the *Meditations* is not to present and later, disprove scepticism. Scepticism for Descartes is only a stepping stone to laying the foundations of his physics.

Historically, scepticism is not Descartes' problem. However, it is still ours. As we saw earlier, Descartes throws us a couple of challenges. In particular, we should be able to either point out the errors in the arguments of the three stages of doubt, or else to embrace their sceptical conclusion. This challenge still stands. We should reply to it. To ignore it seems unfair to Descartes. Moreover, in replying to the challenge, we shall learn some points which will be important in the discussion of the mind/body problem. Consequently, in the appendix, I shall briefly present a reply to the challenge of the First Meditation. However, the reader is urged to try to escape from Descartes' prison for him or herself.

6
The Cogito

Could a malicious demon deceive me into believing that I exist? Descartes thinks not. Suppose a demon is attempting to deceive me about this. Even so, I still cannot doubt that I exist. For, I have to exist in order to be deceived. Consequently, even the possibility of a deceiving demon cannot be a reason for doubting my own existence. I doubt therefore I am. Therefore, I cannot doubt that I am. With these thoughts Descartes ends the phase of doubting and begins the journey of reconstructing knowledge and laying the foundations for his physics.

There is another initial ingredient for this journey. It seems that I cannot be mistaken that I am having an idea while I am having it. Conscious mental states seem to disclose themselves to me in such a way that I cannot be mistaken about them while I am having them. If I think that I am thinking then I am thinking. This means that I cannot be mistaken that I am thinking when I am. For Descartes the word `thought' means a range of mental states such that the person who experiences them is immediately aware of them. The word should not have an intellectual connotation but rather just stands for any conscious mental state. `Thinking' includes doubting, willing, feeling and imagining, and any mental activity of which one is immediately aware.

According to Descartes, the conscious mind is transparent. In today's terminology, according to him, conscious mental states are both evident and incorrigible. They are evident because if I am thinking then I must know that I am. I cannot be ignorant about it. Mental states are incorrigible, because if I believe that I am thinking then it is true that I am thinking. I cannot be mistaken about it. We will examine these two features of the mind in chapter six. For the moment, we are interested in their implications for knowledge, and especially for the Cogito.

In the Cogito, Descartes brings together the two ingredients in the following way. The fact that I am doubting guarantees that I exist. However, doubting is only one type of thought, and thought itself is incorrigible. Thus, I can be certain that I exist merely from the fact that I am thinking, no matter what I am thinking. Therefore, the inference `I doubt therefore I am' can be generalized to `I think therefore I am' or `Cogito ergo sum'. This inference usually called the `Cogito.' The Cogito is special because the premise `I think' is indubitable or incorrigible. This is what distinguishes it from other similar inferences, such as

> I eat green eggs and ham, therefore I am
> I drink, therefore I am
> I walk, therefore I am

These inferences have the same form as the Cogito. The difference between them and the Cogito is that their premises are open to doubt. To have a proof of his existence beyond doubt, Descartes cannot use such premises. He must infer that he exists from the incorrigible fact that he is thinking.

Interpretations of the Cogito

Up to now we have treated the Cogito as a deductive argument from the premise `I am thinking' to the conclusion `I exist.' The conclusion is supposed to be certain, because the inference is valid and the premise is indubitable. However to be valid, this inference would need an additional premise, such as `everything that thinks exists'. The problem is that Descartes apparently denies that the Cogito is such a syllogistic inference. He comments to Mersenne:

> When someone says, `I am thinking therefore I am or exist,' he
> does not deduce existence from thought by a syllogism, but,
> recognizes it as something self-evident by a simple intuition of
> the mind. This is clear from the fact that if he were deducing it
> by means of a syllogism, he would have to have previous
> knowledge of the major premise 'Everything which thinks is,
> or exists'; yet in fact he learns it from experiencing it in his

own case that it is impossible that he should think without
existing. (AT VII 140)

He repeats much the same point to Gassendi (AT IXA 205). Some
interpreters have taken these points to indicate that the Cogito is a
simple appeal to intuition and not an inference at all. Descartes says in
The Rules that everyone can intuit their own existence. According to
this interpretation, the certainty of the Cogito is just a matter of
introspecting or intuiting that one exists.

Is the Cogito an intuition or an inference? The best reply is: both.
First, for Descartes, the difference is a matter of degree anyway. As we
saw in chapter three, in making an inference we intuit the simple
deductive steps. According to Descartes, intuition is required to see that
a conclusion does in fact follow from the premises. Therefore the two
cannot be exclusive. Also, the Cogito requires intuition of the fact that
one is thinking, even if it is an inference. The premise `I am thinking'
has to be intuitively certain if the conclusion `I am' is to be certain.

Second, what is important for Descartes is that the Cogito can be
grasped in one swoop. It is important that I can grasp directly that I
exist. Affirming this does not mean denying the `ergo' in `Cogito ergo
sum'. We can distinguish the Cogito as an inference from the mode of
knowing it. It is an inference which we grasp directly as an intuition.

Descartes regards the connection between thinking and existence
as a necessary one. Consequently, we may suppose that Descartes is
willing to admit `it is impossible to think without existing' as a
presupposition of the Cogito. This does not mean we have to think the
suppressed premise to grasp the Cogito in a flash of intuition.

A Famous Criticism of the Cogito

Some commentators, like Russell, have objected to the occurrence
of the word `I' in the premise `I am thinking'.[1] According to Russell,
Descartes has no right to the premise `I am thinking', but only to the
weaker claim `there is a thought'.[2]

This objection to Descartes' Cogito can be expressed in the form
of a dilemma. Either we believe that what is meant by `I' is an idea of
an 'I' that has thoughts but is not identical with those thoughts; or the 'I'
is simply identical with those thoughts. Either way the Cogito does not
work. If we accept the first alternative, the premise 'I am thinking' will
yield the conclusion 'I exist'. But according to this alternative, 'I am

thinking' is not a suitable premise for the Cogito. The premise of the Cogito is put forward as indubitable, but according to Russell,' I am thinking' is not indubitable. It is open to doubt whether there is an 'I' which thinks and is not identical with these thoughts. Hume, for instance, is one philosopher who challenges this. Since the idea is open to doubt, it is illegitimate for the word `I' to appear in the premise of the Cogito.

If we admit this, and accept the second alternative, there is no justification for the word `I' to appear in the Cogito at all. If what is meant by `I' is simply the occurrence of thought then the premise should be `there is thought'. But from this premise, the conclusion `I exist' cannot be inferred.

Descartes can make two responses to this challenge. First of all, there is good reason for using the word `I' in the premise 'I am thinking'. The reason is that thinking, like green, is a property, and if there is a property there must be something which has this property. That which has a property Descartes calls a substance. There cannot be thinking without there being something which thinks just as, if there is green, there must be something that is green. The existence of a property requires the existence of a substance or thing which has this property. Secondly, Descartes is careful to point out just after the Cogito that he has not yet reached any conclusion about the nature of this `I' which thinks. Even when he is certain that he exists, he has not committed himself to his nature, except that he thinks. Descartes seeks to establish what his essential nature is in the Second Meditation. By the end of that Meditation, he concludes that he is a thing whose essence is to think. However, he does not assume this in the Cogito.

Qualifications

It would be a mistake to think of the Cogito as the basis of Descartes' philosophy. The claim that clear and distinct ideas are true is much more central. However, the Cogito is the turning point. After the Cogito, Descartes' journey goes in two directions:

1. To show that God exists in order to prove the existence of the external world. This line is pursued in Meditations 3 and 5.

2. To show what the essence of the mind is , how it differs from that of matter and thereby prove that the mind is separate from body. This line is pursued in Meditation 2 and 6.

The Cogito is important for the second of these journeys.

7

God Brings the World

How on earth can Descartes prove the existence of the material world? After the Cogito, Descartes' *Meditations* follows two tracks. Along the first, he tries to establish the existence and nature of the physical world. Along the second track, Descartes reveals the nature of the mind and its separation from the body. We shall discuss the second track in chapters seven, eight and nine. The first track is the topic of this and the next chapter.

At the end of the Second Meditation, Descartes has certainty regarding the inner world of his experience. He can be sure of his ideas while he is having them. He can be certain that he exists and that his nature is to think. However, he has still not bridged the gap from this knowledge of his own mind to that of the external world. He cannot be certain that anything in the external world corresponds to, or resembles, his ideas. He knows that there is something out there causing some of his ideas. He can appeal to the principle that everything must have cause. Also some of his ideas do not depend on his own will; these do not seem to be caused by himself. So, they must be caused by something in the external world.

However, up to now, knowledge only extends so far. It does not include yet what the external world consists in or is like. As of yet, Descartes has no evidence to support the hypothesis that his ideas are caused by material objects, as opposed to say a deceiving demon. He cannot claim knowledge regarding the nature of the external world.

Descartes' strategy for bridging the knowledge gap between experience and the world consists in two steps. The first step: he tries to prove the existence of God, with two distinct arguments. He recognizes that these proofs must be based only on knowledge that he has already shown to be certain. He must start from his own idea of God. The second step: Descartes tries to establish that If God exists, then he can treat his own faculties of judgment as reliable and be sure that clear and distinct ideas are true. In this way, Descartes can pass from knowledge of his own ideas to knowledge of the external world.

Step 1: Proving God

Do we have an idea of God? God is infinite and we are finite. Can our finite minds have the idea of something infinite? Both of Descartes' arguments for the existence of God start from the premise that he, Descartes, has this idea. Consequently, he needs to show that we really do have the idea of God, of a perfect, eternal, infinite creator. Descartes' proof uses as a premise the already certain fact that he doubts. To doubt is to lack a perfection, and from the fact that he doubts, he concludes that he is imperfect. Because he has an idea of imperfection, he concludes that he also has an idea of absolute perfection, hence, he has the idea of an absolutely perfect being, i.e. God.

Some of Descartes' contemporaries deny having such an idea. Descartes gives one swift reply to their claim: one need not know that one has this idea in order to have it. To have an idea of God, one is not obliged to conceive of God, for this idea might be an innate capacity. Furthermore, he insists that if the person understands the word `God', then he does have an idea of God.

Gassendi, one of the commentators on the Meditations, argues that even if we use the word `God' meaningfully, this does not show that we have an idea of an infinite perfect being. Gassendi claims that a finite mind cannot comprehend an infinite being. Descartes replies by distinguishing understanding and comprehension. He says that we do have a clear and distinct idea of an infinite being, but no adequate or complete idea of God's infinite being. We understand that God is an infinite being, but we do not comprehend how he is infinite.

THE CAUSAL PROOF OF THE EXISTENCE OF GOD

God Brings the World

The first argument for the existence of God is a causal proof, given in the Third Meditation, and in more detail, in the Discourse. The traditional causal argument for the existence of God is the cosmological argument, which affirms that the only possible cause of the physical universe is God. Descartes cannot give this argument, since he has not yet proven the existence of the physical universe. Instead, Descartes has to start from what he knows for certain. In effect, he argues that the idea of God must have been caused by God. The idea of God is like a trademark, `the mark of the craftsman stamped on his work.' (AT VII 51)

Nothing comes of nothing. Everything has a cause. Descartes accepts this principle of Sufficient Reason as self–evident. According to Descartes, the Principle of Sufficient Reason implies another general proposition, the Principle of Adequate Reality, which claims:

> there must be at least as much reality in the total efficient cause as in the effect.

In other words, if A has less reality than B then B cannot have been caused by A. The Principle of Adequate Reality is implied by the Principle of Sufficient Reason: if the cause had less reality than the effect, then the surplus reality in the effect would be without a cause, and this would contravene the principle that everything must have a cause. To explain the Principle of Adequate Reality, Descartes compares it with heat: heat cannot be induced in a substance except by something at least as hot. You cannot warm your food with an ice-cube.

What are degrees of reality? We can explain Descartes' idea as follows. There are three levels of being: the first floor, properties, such as being white; the second floor, the level of finite substances, such as horses; the third floor, the level of infinite substances.[1] Substances (on the second floor) have more reality that properties (on the first floor) because the existence of properties depends on that of substances. Whiteness exists only in so far as white things exist. In this sense, substances have more reality than properties. In a similar way, God has more reality than any finite substances, because the idea of God is such that finite substances depend for their existence on God.

Note that this does not presuppose that God exists. It just shows us that in the way in which God would exist is different from the way in which finite things and properties exist. Or, to use our analogy, it shows us that there is a third floor. It does not show that there is anything on it. Compare: a unicorn has a higher degree of reality than

45

the color white. However, this does not mean that unicorns actually exist. Similarly, the fact God has a higher degree of reality than finite things does not show that God actually exists. It only shows that if He does exist then His position in the scale of being is on the third level.

We have now explained the Principle of Adequate Reality. To prove that God does exist, Descartes applies the Principle to the content of his ideas or what ideas represent. For example,
- a level 1 idea: the idea of white represents a certain property;
- a level 2 idea: the idea of a unicorn represents a finite substance;
- a level 3 idea: the idea of God represents an infinite substance
When Descartes applies the Principle of Adequate Reality to the content of his ideas, he concludes that an idea needs a cause with at least as much reality as the content of that idea. Every idea must have a cause equal in reality to what it is an idea of. If A has a lesser degree of reality than B, then an idea of B cannot have been caused by A.

This makes the idea of God special. Only God himself has a sufficient degree of reality to cause the idea of God. Consequently, the idea of God could not be caused by anything except God Himself. Descartes is sure that he has an idea of God. Therefore, he concludes that God must exist.

Descartes says that a finite being such as himself could not be the cause of his idea of God, because finite beings possess less reality than God. No finite mind can be adequate to cause the idea of God. As for the idea of external objects, Descartes says `they contain nothing so great that it seems they could not originate from myself'. The idea of an external substance or object could be invented by the mind, because the mind itself is a substance.

We can summarize Descartes' first argument for the existence of God as follows:

1. I have an idea of God
2. This idea must have a cause
3. There cannot be less reality in the cause than in the effect
4. If my idea of God were caused by anything other than God, then there would be less reality in the cause than in the effect
5. Therefore, God exists

The first premise was discussed earlier. The second premise follows from the Principle of Sufficient Reason and the third is the Principle of Adequate Reality.

God Brings the World

The fourth premise results from applying the Principle of Adequate Reality to the content of ideas, or to what they represent. This is clearly the most problematic part of the argument. Despite what Descartes says, we might object that, surely, all ideas at level one. All ideas are properties of minds, and as properties they all belong on the first floor, whatever content they might have. In this way the idea of God is no different from that of a unicorn, and therefore requires no special cause.

Descartes applies the Principle to the content of ideas. In the *Principles*, he supports this application with an appeal to the idea of a complex machine (AT VIII 11). Suppose a person has the idea of a complicated machine. Where has he obtained this idea from? Either he has seen such a machine made by someone else, or he has the sophistication or complexity of mind sufficient to have thought of it himself. The intricacy or complexity of the content of the idea must also be contained in its cause. Because of this kind of consideration, Descartes believes that the cause of an idea must have at least as much reality as what the idea represents

(Note that in his texts Descartes uses scholastic terminology which is confusing for us today. He contrasts the objective and formal properties of ideas. He does not use the terms 'objective' and 'formal' in their usual contemporary sense. The phrase 'the objective properties of an idea' stands for the content of the idea. The objective properties of an idea are the properties it has as a representation. My idea of a unicorn has the objective property of being of the idea of a substance. The formal properties of the idea are those it has a mode of someone's consciousness, as an event in the real world. As we have seen, Descartes argues that the Principle of Adequate Reality should be applied to the content of ideas or to what they are ideas of. Descartes expresses this point by saying that the principle should be applied to the objective. rather than just to the formal properties of ideas.)

What should we think of this first argument for the existence of God ? First, there is an ambiguity in the notion of 'degrees of reality'. Whereas modes are logically dependent on the existence of substances, created substances are only causally dependent on God. Consequently there is no uniform property of `reality' that things possess in varying degrees. Modes are dependent on substances in a different way from that in which created substances are supposed to be dependent on God.

We might also challenge Descartes' Principle of Adequate Reality on other grounds. But more important, even if we grant that principle to Descartes, there are problems with the way he specifically applies it to ideas. In order for Descartes to arrive at his desired conclusion, namely that the idea of God must be caused by God, it is not sufficient for him to apply the principle to ideas merely as modes of consciousness (i.e.. to their formal properties). As a mode of consciousness the idea of God has the same degree of reality as any other idea; it is merely a property of a substance, a mind. As a mode of consciousness the idea of God, like any other idea, need only be caused by a finite substance; it could be invented by the mind. In order to obtain his desired conclusion, Descartes must apply the Principle of Adequate Reality to the content of his ideas (i.e.. to their objective properties). This is the crucial turning point of his argument, yielding the required premise 4: the cause of an idea must have as much reality as what the idea is of. But why should we accept this special application of the principle? In answer to this, Descartes only has the analogy with the idea of a complex machine, which is a weak argument.

The analogy with complex machines can be used to articulate another problem with the argument. We should distinguish the blue–print of such a machine, which requires skill in the cause, from a child's drawing of the machine, which does not. Our idea of God might be like the child's drawing rather than the blue–print. Descartes' argument requires that we should have a positive idea of an infinite being. But perhaps our idea of God is not like that. For instance, it could be the idea of a being who does not have the imperfections and limitations that we have. Such an idea might be abstracted from knowledge of our own limitations and imperfections. The having of such an idea would not require the existence of God as its cause. This might be called a negative idea of God. With this line of argument, even if we accept the special application of the principle of adequate reality outlined above, we can deny that this proves the existence of God.

The Ontological Argument

In the Fifth Meditation, Descartes offers a simpler proof for the existence of God. Whereas the first argument was a causal one, the second is an ontological argument based on the nature of God's essence, originally from St. Anselm. The essence of a thing consists in its essential properties, of what is necessarily contained in the idea of that thing. The essence of a triangle is to have three sides. An idea of a

thing that did not have this property could not be the idea of a triangle.
Usually knowledge of the essence of a thing does not inform us of that thing's existence. Usually essence and existence are distinct. However, Descartes argues that, in the case of God, the two coincide. The essence of God involves His existence. The idea of God is of a being with every perfection (or good quality). According to Descartes, existence is a perfection. For which would be the better: a perfect being who does not exist, or one who does? The latter is better. Consequently, existence is a good quality and since God has all good qualities, it follows that He exists. If God did not exist then He would lack a perfection, which is impossible.

1. By definition, God, if He exists, has all perfections
2. Existence is a perfection
3. Therefore, God exists.

An important criticism of this argument, made famous later by Kant, is that premise 2 is false because existence is not a property of things at all. The sentence `John is tall' attributes a property to an individual, but the sentence `John exists' does not. To deny that John exists is not to deny that he has a certain attribute. As Gassendi says in the Objections, 'something which does not exist is neither perfect nor imperfect'.

One way to see that existence is not a property at all is to show that the claim would have absurd consequences. If existence were a property, comparable to green, then some things would have it and others would not. Those things which lack the property of existence could be called merely possible objects. For instance, how many brothers could you have had? According to this idea, there are an indefinite number of merely possible brothers which do not actually exist. However, this claim implies that most brothers do not exist. `Existence is a predicate' implies that most brothers do not exist. Since this consequence is absurd, we should deny that existence is a property.

Furthermore, there are no clear criteria for the identification or individuation of merely possible objects. To use an example from Quine, we cannot decide whether the possible bald man in the doorway is the same as or different from the possible fat man in the doorway.[2] For identity, it is necessary that we be able to tell when two predications are made of the same thing, but we cannot do this with possible objects. Once the idea of merely possible objects has been discredited, there is no case for treating existence as a property.

Step 2: Reconstructing Knowledge

Descartes' strategy for escaping the prison of his own ideas is to demonstrate the following principle:

BP: Clear and distinct ideas are true.

We may call this the bridge principle, because it serves as a bridge between the realm of private ideas and the external world. Remember that at this stage of the argument, Descartes can only be certain of his own ideas. Therefore, he needs some principle which establishes what the external world is like, but solely on the basis of how ideas seem to the subject. The bridge principle does this, for whether an idea is clear and distinct depends solely on how it strikes the mind or how it feels. In other words, if an idea is clear and distinct then I can know that it is so, while I am having the idea. An idea is clear is one which is present and open to the attentive mind; a distinct idea contains nothing unclear (AT VIII 22).

The general principle that clear and distinct ideas are true, furnishes us with a way of avoiding error. We must always suspend our assent to ideas which are unclear and indistinct. The question of whether one gives assent to an idea or judges it to be true is a matter for the will. The first step is establishing the bridge principle was to argue for the existence of God. The second step is to demonstrate the second premise of the argument below.

1. God exists
2. If God exists then clear and distinct ideas are true
3. Therefore clear and distinct ideas are true

Because God is a perfect being, `God is liable to no errors or defects'. Therefore, He is not a deceiver and would not wish us to be lead into error. Thus we can be sure that our clear and distinct ideas are true.

The mere existence of mental images and sensations gives us no reason to think that there are objects corresponding to them. Nevertheless, we have a very strong natural tendency to believe in the existence of a world of material objects and that our ideas are caused by it, and this tendency survives the scrutiny of reason. So, if sensations were in general not caused by such a reality, we would be deceived by God, which is impossible. Descartes carefully notes that this does not mean that all objects are as we perceive them to be, for perception may be obscure and confused in many ways.

By the Sixth Meditation, Descartes has restored his knowledge of the world and has answered the doubts of the First Meditation. From his search, he has gained much.

First, he has learned that sense experience on its own is not at all a reliable way to gain knowledge. Sense experience has to be vindicated by Reason. It is reasoning which shows when, and in what way, sense perception is reliable. Descartes does not have to abandon sense perception as a source of knowledge, but neither is he forced to rely on it unquestioningly. Reason is the primary source of knowledge.

Secondly, the search has given Descartes important methodological principles to guide further inquiry. In particular, he knows that he can trust clear and distinct ideas, and that he must withhold assent to confused and indistinct ones. This will be important for Descartes in establishing the basis of his physics.

Thirdly, the unwritten aim of reconciling the new science with religion has been partly achieved. A proper scientific study of nature must be grounded in clear methodological principles, but these principles require us to show that God exists. In this respect at least, science cannot be a challenge to religion for true science requires the existence of God.

Fourthly, after completing this part of his search, Descartes has a quite different vision of how the material world actually is. For example, as we shall in the next chapter, he has learned that things are not really colored and he will establish what the real essence of matter is.

This is the way to go forward. However, before that, we must consider two problems with Descartes' strategy. First, there is the complaint that he has argued in a circle, begging the question. Second, there is argument that he has rendered false beliefs impossible.

The Cartesian Circle

Earlier Descartes seemed to be locked in the realm of his own ideas unable to show whether any of them represented external reality. Having now proved the existence of God, he can be sure that when he assents to a clear and distinct idea he will have a true belief. For God would not deceive us about what seems clear and obvious to us. Descartes has often been accused of arguing in a circle here. Arnauld expresses the circle as follows:

..we can be sure that God exists only because we clearly and
evidently perceive that He does; therefore prior to being
certain that God exists, we should be certain that whatever we
perceive clearly and distinctly is true.

If Descartes uses the principle `whatever is distinctly and clearly
perceived is true' in his proof of God, he cannot also use God to
establish the truth of that principle. That would be to argue in a circle.

There are two ways to reply on Descartes' behalf. First, we could
point out that Descartes has two proofs for the existence of God which
do not explicitly depend on the claim that clear and distinct ideas are
true. It is not a premise of either of the two arguments. In this way,
Descartes can prove God without first explicitly affirming that clear
and distinct ideas are true.

Second, the reply to the above is that Descartes must implicitly
rely on the claim that clear and distinct ideas are true in order to able to
deduce at all. To defend Descartes against this point, to show that
Descartes does not even implictly argue in a circle, we should return to
the nature of doubt. According to Descartes one `cannot but assent' to a
clear and distinct idea whilst thinking it: he says of these ideas `we
cannot think of them without at the same time believing them to be
true'. Clear and distinct ideas cannot be doubted while we have them.
But this seems to contravene the Method of Doubt, although in fact it
does not. It seems to contravene the Method of Doubt because among
the ideas doubted were clear and distinct ones; for instance, the
proposition `2 + 2 = 4' forms a clear and distinct idea but mathematics
came under the ambit of doubt. In fact, the Method of Doubt does not
involve doubting the clear and distinct ideas at the time of thinking
them. In doubting the propositions of mathematics, Descartes does not
raise specific doubts about the proposition `2 + 2 = 4' but about the
class of mathematical propositions as a whole. The Method of Doubt
does not involve doubting particular clear and distinct ideas, but a
general systematic scepticism about the reliability of our judgements
and faculties as a whole.[3]

We can now see how Descartes avoids the charge of circularity.
He never offers the existence of God as a ground for accepting the truth
of particular clear and distinct perceptions or intuitions. According to
him the clarity of intuition is good enough. So when Descartes uses the
truth of particular clear intuitions to prove the existence of God, he is
not arguing in a circle. He does not also use the existence of God to

establish the truth of those particular clear intuitions.

Although clear and distinct beliefs cannot be doubted at the time of our having them, there remains the `metaphysical possibility' that the faculty of intuition as a whole might be mistaken. The existence of God is used by Descartes to allay this general and systematic doubt. God is introduced not to establish the principle `what is clearly and distinctively perceived is true'. God is introduced to meet general systematic doubts about the truth of clear ideas. This is not circular. Descartes uses the truth of particular clear ideas to establish the existence of God, and thus to vindicate the general trustworthiness of intuition as a whole. Suppose I am having a clear and distinct idea now. Whilst I am having this idea, I am sure that it is true. But there is a problem: holding on to the idea is difficult and when it is not intuited anymore, I can no longer be sure that it is true. However, this problem is solved once I know that God exists, because then I can be sure of my clear and distinct ideas, even when I am not intuiting or having them. Descartes says to Burman that the proof of God can be grasped in a single thought. Once we clearly perceive that God exists and that he is no deceiver, we can allay systematic doubts about intuition in general.

False beliefs

God guarantees that clear and distinct ideas are true. Descartes knows that God would not deceive him. God would not have given him a faculty that leads him astray. Once Descartes can be sure of this, he has a methodological principle to guide all enquiry, a way to avoid error. However, given that God is an all-powerful, benevolent, all-perfect being, how is it possible to ever make any mistakes? If God is all-perfect, then surely, we would not fall into error at all; yet we do. Why doesn't the Divine guarantee of the Third Meditation rule out all false beliefs?

In the Fourth Meditation Descartes tries to solve this problem by explaining what error is. This account of error is an important part of Descartes' whole project, since this understanding would help us avoid error, in so far as we can.

Descartes does not intend to investigate why God should have created him imperfect, for Descartes thinks it would be rash and fruitless to inquire into the aims of God. Descartes intends to investigate what human limitation causes errors.

Descartes divides all thoughts into two kinds: ideas and volitions.

Ideas are like images, because they represent: e.g. the idea of the house on the hill. However, ideas themselves are neither true nor false; they have to be judged as true for there to be any possibility of error. Consequently, the need for the second type of thought, volition.

Volitions are roughly what one does with ideas. They are mental attitudes and in the Third Meditation Descartes cites four kinds of such volitions: to desire, fear, affirm and deny. Fearing and desiring are acts of the will. Affirming and denying are two kinds of judging, which involve opposite mental attitudes towards a proposition and, according to Descartes, are acts of the will too.

According to this view, Descartes claims that all mental acts consists of two elements: a mental attitude towards an idea. In contemporary terminology, mental acts, such as judging, consist of two distinct aspects combined: a propositional attitude and a propositional content. According to Descartes corresponding to these two elements, there are two faculties: understanding, which produces the propositional content, and the will, which affirms or denies it. To Regius, Descartes writes: "Understanding is properly the passive aspect of the mind; and willing its active aspect." (ATIII 372)

So, according to Descartes, belief involves judging which is an act of will. Is this plausible? Should we think of belief as an act of will? Surely, what we believe is not up to us in this way. Usually we do not decide what to believe. The reply: Descartes' theory is not that we decide what to believe. There is no prior act of decision.[4] Instead, his theory is that believing involves an act of the will.

Descartes' two pronged account of judgment might explain why beliefs can have different intensities and why beliefs can be more or less firm. It also explains how Descartes views intellectual training: as an exercise of the will. More importantly, it explains how error is possible.

Mistaken beliefs are possible when the understanding and the will are mismatched. Neither the understanding nor the will on their own are the cause of error. According to Descartes, error originates because 'my will extends more widely than my understanding, and yet I do not restrain it within the same bounds, but apply it to what I do not understand'. In other words, error comes about because the will is limitless and the understanding is limited and the will assents to ideas that are not properly understood.

The problem of false beliefs is a little like the famous problem of evil. In both cases, the problem is, how could an all-perfect God allow it? (i.e. in the one case, how can an all perfect God allow evil? and in the other, How can He allow error?) The traditional solution to the problem of evil is the appeal to free will. Descartes answer to his problem of error also resorts to free-will. Errors are false judgments and judgments are acts of will. In making judgments, I must be careful to exercise the freedom God has given me properly by giving my assent only to ideas which are clear and distinct. This is my responsibility. God guarantees that my faculties are generally trustworthy in the sense that my clear and distinct ideas will be true. This is God's responsibility. Consequently it is impossible to make false judgments, but only if one uses the faculties correctly. Descartes says that the fact that errors do occur points to "some imperfection in me" (ATVII 56).

8
Matter

Descartes' scientific interests were wide and varied. When he first moved to Holland in 1629, his interests shifted from mathematics to natural philosophy. His first interest in physics was in optics and the principles of refraction. His essay on Optics was published in 1637 and contains an early version of what is now called Snell's law. Since his early days in Paris, Descartes had planned the construction of a machine to make lenses without aberrations. From this first seed, other concerns quickly grew. He became interested in light and his new unified conception of the physical world quickly took a definite shape. He also became interested in the workings of the body and worked on anatomy, dissecting carcasses purchased in local butchers' shops.

Descartes' system turns on the idea that the physical universe consists only of matter and its spatio-temporal properties. Descartes claims that the whole essence of matter consists in its being extended in space. The essence of matter consists only in such properties as shape, size and motion.

To show that the essence of matter is solely spatial extension, Descartes argues that a body can lose any of its properties, except extension, without ceasing to be a material body. The essence of a thing consists in the properties without which that thing would cease to exist. The essence is what that thing must have. At Principles II, 11 he claims that a body can lose hardness, weight, color and heat without ceasing to be a body. Since it cannot lose extension, extension is the essential attribute of material bodies. From this simple starting point, we can understand many of Descartes' views regarding scientific matters: explanation, the unity of the sciences and methodology.

1) Explanation

According to Descartes, all physical changes should be explained solely in terms of extension. This is a simple but revolutionary change. Scholastic philosophers were used to explaining changes in terms of occult forms or qualities. Eustacius, a 17th century scholastic, wrote:

> There are individual behaviors appropriate to each individual natural thing, as reasoning is to human beings, neighing to horses, heating to fire, and so on. But these behaviors do not arise from matter .... They must arise from the substantial form.[1]

To use an example from *The World*, the scholastics would have said that wood burns because it has the form of being combustible. Descartes wants undermine the foundations of Scholaticism, without becoming embroiled in the arguments between different scholastic schools. Descartes realizes that there are three problems with scholastic explanation. First, it does not explain anything to say that wood burns because it has the property of being flammable. Descartes says that the forms themselves need to be explained. It does not explain what makes wood flammable. Second, it is ontologically extravagant to postulate these forms or qualities as entities in addition to matter. Third, Descartes complains that the normal scholastic explanation amounts to the attribution of "a tiny mind" to inanimate bodies (AT III 648) . For example, they think of heaviness as something mental - a substance linked to a body that "bears bodies toward the center of the earth as if it contains some thought of it (i.e. the center of the earth) within itself (AT VII 442). In other words, scholasticism projects mental ideas into the material world.

Descartes replaces the scholastic view with the idea of mechanical explanation in terms of the extension of the parts of things. Since all matter is of the same kind and is governed by the same laws, the differing reactions of bodies must be explained in terms of the differing size, shape and motion of the smaller bodies (corpuscles) that make them up. Descartes thinks that with a few simple principles, we can

57

show that `the stars and the earth, and everything else we can observe on the earth, could have developed as if from seeds.' He says: "And because all natural phenomena can be thus explained ... I think that no other principles of physics should be accepted" (P II, 64).

2) The unity of the sciences

In the preface to the Principles, Descartes compares knowledge to a tree: "the roots are metaphysics; the trunk is physics, and the branches emerging from the trunk are all the other sciences which may be reduced to three principal ones: medicine, mechanics and morals." The general laws of nature, which form the trunk of philosophy, can be deduced from the metaphysical foundation, the roots. For example, the first law of motion (that every material object continues in motion or at rest unless some cause affects it) can be deduced from the principle of sufficient reason.

Descartes was convinced of the unity of knowledge from very early on, at least from 1619. In the Rules, he argues against those who "think that each science should be studied separately, without regard to any of the others" (AT X 360). Such an attitude prevents one from looking for general explanatory principles. Given the uniform nature of matter and of the laws governing it, the unity of science seems to follow.

3) Methodology

In Part VI of the Discourse, Descartes summarizes his method:

> First I tried to discover in general the principles or first causes
> of everything....Next I examined the first and most ordinary
> effects deducible from these causes... Then when I sought to
> descend to more particular things, I encountered such a variety
> that.. (I had)..to make use of many special observations. (AT
> VI 63)

As we have just seen, Descartes thinks that the most general laws of nature can be derived by reasoning from the most fundamental metaphysical principles, which themselves are established rationally. For example, Descartes derives two of his laws of motion from the immutable nature of God: the laws of conservation of quantity of motion, of the persistence of size, shape and rectilinear motion and the laws of impact. This is why natural philosophy requires a metaphysical foundation.

However, this does not mean that observation has no role in science. Descartes' own life was dedicated to experimental observation in all areas of science, despite his views about the confused nature of sense perception. Moreover, his own explanation of scientific methodology explains the need for experiments. The extraordinary variety of natural things requires us to make observation. Furthermore, at the level of the particular, we need to frame hypotheses and test them against experience and observation, because of the nature of explanation. There could be several competing alternative explanations of why something happens. Descartes says that "to explain, it suffices to imagine a cause which could produce the effect in question, even if it could have been produced by other causes and we do not know which is the true cause" (5 Oct. 1646). To see which of the possible explanations is actually effective in a particular case, we need to observe.

The Meditations give the metaphysical grounds for Descartes' natural philosophy or physics. What does this consist in? First and foremost, it consists in the claim that the whole essence of matter is extension. We have just examined some of the fundamental implications of this claim. Second, this claim is supported by Descartes' theory of clear and distinct ideas. He asserts that material bodies "possess all the properties that I clearly and distinctly understand, that is .. all those which come within the subject matter of pure mathematics." (AT VII 80) In other words, we can understand material objects clearly and distinctly when we grasp them under the geometrical properties of extension. This ensures the science of matter can and should consist in quantifiable laws. In claiming that matter is extension, Descartes supports his mathematical view of science. For extension and motion are obviously quantifiable and measurable. This means that they are distinct and clear ideas.

Implications

Descartes' conception of matter as extension has some radical consequences. First, it implies that a vacuum is impossible. Descartes argues that matter as extension and physical space are identical, and hence, there can be no empty space. He also argues that a vacuum is impossible because if there is nothing between two bodies then they must be in contact (see Principles II 18). Secondly, his conception of matter also implies that there are no indivisible atoms. All parts of matter must be extended and anything that is extended is, like space, infinitely divisible (see Principles II 20). Thirdly, Descartes holds that all properties of matter must be explained in terms of matter in motion. But since there is no vacuum for bodies to move into, `the only possible movement of bodies is in a circle'. As one part of matter moves, it pushes another out of the place it enters, and this pushes another and so on, until a body enters the place left by the first body `at the very moment the first body leaves it'. Fourthly, Descartes' view of matter excludes force and solidity as basic. However, he does hold as logical truth that two things cannot be in the same place at the same time, so that matter occupying one part of space excludes other matter from occupying the same place. For Descartes, weight is not an intrinsic property either: it is the force of the motion of a body.

Due to his conception of physical science, Descartes pictures the material world as one continuous, infinite, extended whole. This anticipates Spinoza's view that there is only one substance. Thus, while there are an indefinite number of mental substances, strictly speaking, there is only one extended substance, the material universe as a whole. Particular objects can be distinguished only by differences in motion and matter at different places. Objects are differentiated as different ways in which matter moves. Or as Kenny puts it `"one body" just means as much of matter as moves together.' [2]

PRIMARY AND SECONDARY QUALITIES

There is one further important consequence of Descartes' view of matter. This is the distinction which Locke later called the primary/secondary quality distinction. According to this, so called secondary qualities, such as heat, sound, taste, colors and flavors, are not properties of objects at all. They are only confused ideas that exist in the mind due to its interaction with the body. Strictly speaking, matter is not colored at all. Descartes writes: "by means of the senses, we apprehend nothing in external objects beyond their shapes, sizes and motions." (AT VIII 321) Light, color, odor, sound, heat and cold are merely dispositions of the objects to cause certain motions in our nerves. For example, the tree itself has only extended properties. When we perceive a tree as colored, some variation in the extended properties of the tree cause in us the idea of green. The tree itself is not colored but only has the power to cause in us the idea or sensation of color.

One of Descartes' reasons for holding this view is that secondary qualities are not clear and distinct ideas. To judge that the tree is itself green is to assent to a confused idea. In this, Descartes contrasts the ideas of color with the clear and quantifiable ideas of extension and motion. In the *Principles* he affirms that thinking that the object itself is colored is like judging that pain is something real, existing outside of the mind (AT VIIIA 33).

Another reason for Descartes' view is his belief that secondary qualities have no role in an adequate physiological account of perception. Perception can be fully explained in terms of the effect of matter in motion upon the mind. Furthermore, Descartes' conception of physical reality is that of the world as it really is or as it is independently of observers. This notion of the world as it really is should be contrasted with that of the world as it seems to us. Given such a contrast, it is natural to exclude colors and other secondary qualities from the world as it really is.[3] This is because our experience of colors is dependent on physiological factors that are peculiar to us as a species. For example, dogs do not see color. The so-called primary qualities on the other hand, do not seem to be species or individual relative in the same way. For these reasons color and other secondary qualities are often excluded from a scientific picture of the world as it really is, whereas the primary qualities like shape, size, and motion are included.

9

Animals and Machines

After causing you to wonder at the most powerful machines,
the most unusual automata, the most impressive illusions and
the most subtle tricks that human ingenuity can devise, I shall
reveal to you the secrets behind them which are so simple and
straightforward that you will no longer have reason to wonder
at anything made by the hands of man. I shall then pass to the
works of nature, and after showing you the cause of all her
changes, the variety of her qualities...I shall present for your
consideration, the entire edifice of the things which are
perceivable by the senses.

These are the words of Eudoxus, Descartes' mouthpiece in his
unfinished dialogue, the *Search for the Truth*. Descartes' idea is this:
Nature is a complex mechanism; so then are the animals which are a
part of nature. For this reason, they may be compared with clockwork.
Real birds are comparable to the toy mechanical birds on show in the
circus. The difference is one of degree, not one of principle. In the
Description of the Human Body, Descartes writes:

> I shall try to give such a full account of the entire bodily machine that we shall have no more reason to think that it is our soul which produces the movements. which are not controlled by the will than we have reason to think that there is a soul in a clock which makes it tell the time. (AT XI 226)

Gaukroger tells an extraordinary story about Descartes.[1] In the 18th and 19th centuries there was in circulation the following gossip: in later life Descartes was accompanied by a mechanical, life size, female doll, whom he had constructed to show that animals have no souls. The gossip said that Descartes named the doll after his illegitimate daughter Francine, and that the two were indistinguishable. Apparently this story was put about as a reaction to the (actually false) claim that Descartes had secretly held a mechanistic and materialist account of the mind, extending his view of animals to humans.

With regard to animals, it seems that Descartes gives a causal account of mental states. He does not deny that animals have mental states. He actually affirms that they have sense perceptions and can imagine. Leaving aside the question of whether animals can be conscious according to Descartes, it is clear that he thinks that certain animal mental states can be explained mechanically. This is one model of mental states- the causal account.

The other model is the one that Descartes is more famous today: the introspectivist account of mental states. This is his account of conscious mental states, applicable to rational beings such as us humans. In this vein, Descartes writes in the Second Meditation: "I see clearly that there is nothing easier for me to know than my own mind." These words not only define Descartes' epistemological problem (how to go from knowledge of ideas to knowledge of objects), but they also characterize his view of mental states. Ideas are the objects of immediate perception and the mind is what has these ideas. How ideas are perceived defines what they are.

In this chapter we shall explain the relation between these two very different views of mental states - the introspectivist and the causal. Descartes' dualism and his ontology of the mind is for the next chapter.

The Essence of the Mind

Let us put this in the context of the text. In the Second Meditation, after the `Cogito', Descartes is sure of his own existence. However, at this stage, he is not yet sure of much else. He is not sure yet that he has a body, because external objects are still in doubt. Also, he is not certain what he is. His next step is to discover what his essential nature is. In the Second Meditation, he argues that he is a thinking being and that his essence is to think.

By `thought' he means a range of conscious mental states such that he who experiences them is immediately aware of them. It includes any mental activity of which one is immediately aware. By `essence' he means the properties that a substance must have. To cease to have an essential property is to cease to exist.

In the Second Meditation Descartes argues that his essence is to think, because it is inconceivable that he should not think. He seems to move directly from the `Cogito' to the claim that his essence is to think as follows:

    (1) I cannot conceive of myself not thinking
    (2) I cannot exist without thinking

The argument is that 1) implies 2). The problem is that 1) means a) In order to conceive of myself, I have to think, which is quite different from the premise need to derive 2), namely b) It is impossible to conceive of myself as a being who is not thinking.

In the Second Meditation Descartes claims that his essence is to think. In the Sixth Meditation, he argues for the stronger claim that the whole of his essence is to think. His only essential attribute is thought. The mind has one and only one essential property or attribute. This means that all properties of the mind are simply modes or modifications of its essential attribute, thought. All properties of the mind are only different types of thought.

In this way, Descartes' view of the mind parallels his view of matter. As we saw in the previous chapter, according to Descartes, the whole essence of matter consists in extension. All properties of matter are simply modes of extension. Now Descartes is making a similar claim about the mind and thought. On the 2nd May 1644 he writes:

> The difference between the soul and its ideas is exactly like that between a piece of wax and its diverse shapes that it can receive. (AT IV 113)

In the Sixth Meditation, Descartes argues for the claim that his whole essence is thought. In the Sixth Meditation he can employ the principle that clear and distinct ideas are true, which was unavailable in the Second. He argues that he can see clearly and distinctly that for each property other than thought, it is possible for him to exist without that property. [2]

> I do not remark that any other thing necessarily pertains to my nature or essence, excepting that I am a thinking thing, I rightly conclude that my essence consists solely in the fact that I am a thinking thing.

He has a clear and distinct idea of himself as a thinking thing and that idea includes no perception of himself being anything else. Consequently, his sole essence is to think.

Later on in the Sixth Meditation, Descartes uses these claims to argue for dualism, the ontological theory that mind and body are distinct things. However, we should separate Descartes' ontological dualism (the subject matter of the next chapter) from his views about the nature of the mind and of consciousness (the subject of this chapter).

Two Aspects of Thought

Thought has two aspects. Descartes expresses the point by saying that the term `idea' is ambiguous. Sometimes it should "be taken materially for an operation of the intellect." Alternatively, it can be taken "objectively for the thing which is represented by this operation.. even if it is not supposed to exist outside the intellect." (AT VII 8)

The first aspect consists in the mental acts or events which take place in the mind. According to Descartes, there are two different kinds of mental act: perception and willing. The same division applies to individual thoughts: perceptions and volitions. The main difference is that we are passive with respect to perceptions and active with regard to willing. In this sense of the term, ideas are conscious events in the mind.

The second aspect consists in the content or mental objects of those operations. In this sense, an idea is what is represented or thought or willed. They are the objects of consciousness. [3]

These two aspects of the mind require each other. Every mental act or event must have a content or a mental object. Similarly, mental objects cannot exist apart from some act of thought. In Descartes' idiom, in the material sense of the term `idea', all ideas represent something and what is represented by them is always an idea, in the

65

objective sense of the term.

In other words, according to Descartes, whenever anyone thinks, the thought has an object and this object is something in the thinker's mind. When I think of the moon, my thought has two aspects: the conscious thinking itself and the idea I thinking of. As we saw in Chapter 4, Descartes argues vigorously for a radical distinction between the idea and what the idea is supposed to represent in the world. I must distinguish between my idea and the moon itself. My thinking represents something even if the moon itself does not exist. Therefore, it represents an idea of the moon. In other words, what I perceive is not the moon itself, but the idea of the moon.

the Introspective Account

According to Descartes, the content of mental states or ideas should be defined by how they are perceived by the person who has them. We may call this introspectivism or the introspective account of the content of mental states, because it affirms that mental states are defined by their introspective feel. Descartes by defining ideas as the immediate object of perception. This appears to be a subjective and essentially private definition of mental states. Pain is pain because of the way it feels to the person undergoing it.

This introspective account of the content of mental contents or ideas implies that mental states are both evident and incorrigible:

* Evident because if I am thinking then I must know that I am. I cannot be ignorant about it.

* Incorrigible, because if I believe that I am thinking then it is true that I am thinking. I cannot be mistaken about it.

These two claims seem to be correct for paradigm examples of mental states. For example, the thought "Tomorrow it will hot and I will go to the beach." It seems that I could not be mistaken or ignorant about having this thought. We might say that such mental states seem to be fully present to consciousness in the sense that you could not be mistake or ignorant about them.

However, not all mental states fit this paradigm. For example, you are lost in a day-dream. You find yourself driving to the bank and you realize that you must have been thinking that you need money. Another example: often we are mistaken about what we really want.

The Causal Analysis of Mind

Some mental states do not seem to fit into Descartes' introspectivist paradigm. However, causal or functional theories of the mind claim that the whole introspectivist paradigm is mistaken. The alternative is that mental states should be identified and defined through their causal role. For example, pain has certain potential effects on behavior and typical types of causes. This is what identifies it as pain. To be in pain is to be in a state which would cause such and such behavior or actions. Any mental state has a range of potential effects on behavior given certain conditions (e.g. how an angry person would behave if they were uninhibited). These dispositions are part of its causal role, which define that mental state. Also, sensations are often identified by their typical public causes (e.g. the sensation you get when you hear a chalk board being scratched). More generally, a mental state is defined by its causal role: as a dispositional state to behave in certain ways under certain conditions due to certain causes.

Functionalism offers a causal analysis of the content of mental states, which takes into account the interconnections between mental states. Functionalism identifies mental states partly by their causal role with respect to other mental states, and in this way, it avoids the problems of simplistic behaviorism. A functionalist would define a mental state as a disposition to act and have other mental states, given certain sensory inputs and mental states.

The functionalist account gives us a way to think about the content of mental states which recognizes the need for objective and public criteria for mental states. This is a major difference between it and the introspective approach, which provides an essentially first-person and subjective criterion. This difference we shall examine later in the chapter.

Descartes and the Animals

Are birds conscious? Are they aware of the environment around them? Surely, they are. Although Descartes denies that animals have minds, he certainly thinks that they have some mental states. In a letter of November 1646, he writes:

> All the things which dogs, horses and monkeys are taught to perform are only the expression of their fear, their hope or their joy.. (AT IV 574)

This implies that, for Descartes, animals do have feelings, even though they do not have a non-material mind or soul. We may conclude:

a) According to Descartes, some mental states can be purely physically based and mechanically explained. This is because animals, which have no soul and which have bodies that are highly complex machines, have some mental states. Therefore, such mental states can be accounted for according to the causal or functionalist view.

b) Other mental states, such as thoughts, cannot be so treated, because they require the existence of a non-material mind. These mental states must be accounted for according to the introspectivist account.

This raises two interesting questions: where does Descartes draw the line between these two kinds of mental states? And on what basis? Textually, there are two different answers to the first question.

1) The first: animals can have passions and perceptual ideas insofar these are merely bodily changes. Because they lack a soul, animals cannot have any conscious experiences. Therefore, they do not have the conscious experiences involved in the having of passions and ideas. Consciousness requires the presence of a non-material mind.

2) The second: animals can have the conscious experience of passions and perceptual ideas. Because they lack a soul, animals cannot have self-consciousness. An animal can be aware, but it cannot be aware of its awareness. Self-awareness requires the presence of a non-material mind.

Which one of these is more likely to be Descartes' considered answer? On the basis of the texts, it is difficult to tell. Let us leave the point undecided. The second reply squares more with our intuitions about other animals, but it would have the interesting implication that Descartes is committed to a causal/functionalist account of consciousness (though not self-consciousness).

In either case, Descartes draws the line on the basis of language and understanding. Descartes would admit that it would be possible to construct a mechanical automata which would be behaviorally indistinguishable from any animal. In the case of a human, however, a mechanistic replica would be impossible because

It is not conceivable that such a machine should produce different arrangements of words so as to give an appropriately meaningful answer to whatever is said in its presence, as the dullest of men can do. (AT VI 56)

In part V of the Discourse, he also says that a machine would reveal that it was not acting through understanding, because inevitably, it would fail to do as well as humans in some tasks, even though in others it might excel. In other words, a computer might do well at playing chess or composing music, but there would be some task that it would be unable to perform (such as making peace between two squabbling relatives). The machine would lack reason which "is a universal instrument which can be used in all kinds of situations." (AT VI 56) According to Descartes, these are the two overt signs by which we can distinguish a being which has a soul from one which does not.

No Sharp Lines

According to Descartes, there is a sharp dividing line between the souled human and the mechanical, souless animal or machine. This line is consists in language and reason.

Recent advances in the study of animal behavior and in artificial intelligence challenge the very idea of such a sharp dividing line. For example, it appears that it is possible to teach chimpanzees and gorillas sign language. The apes use the sign language in way that shows some complex linguistic abilities. For example, their use shows some syntactical structure. There is a difference between, "I hit you" and "You hit me". This difference is signified by the positioning of the words, which apparently the apes are able to differentiate. Another characteristic of our linguistic abilities is that we are able to use old words in new circumstances. The monkeys can do this. Not only can they use old worlds in new situations, but they can also create new words. For example, Koko called a grapefruit a "yellow orange."

In general, it seems that the difference between obviously mechanical behavior and the kind of adaptable intelligent behavior mentioned by Descartes is one of degree, not one of kind. If some of the basic claims of artificial intelligence are correct, the difference is merely a question of complexity.

Apparently where Descartes sees a difference in kind between humans and other animals, there are only differences of degree. If so, then his introspectivist view of human mental states is open to a slippery slope objection. If we can give a functionalist account of the mental states of birds and monkeys, then the same should apply to humans, who lack linguistic ability. If we can give a functionalist account of the mental states of apes with some linguistic abilities, then the same kind of analysis should apply to humans with impoverished linguistic capacities. In other words, if there are only differences of degree then the functionalist analysis should apply to humans too.

Publicity

On the one hand, Descartes has an approach to the mental states of animals which would be quite consistent with functionalism. On the other hand, he has an introspectivist approach to the mental state of persons.

Are there reasons to favor one account over the other for conscious mental states? This is an important debate within contemporary philosophy of mind, which we will briefly review to better understand the strengths and weaknesses of Descartes' view.

The causal, functional analysis links the definition of mental states to their potential outer manifestations, which are public and objective. This is in contrast to the introspective analysis which treats mental states as essentially private and subjective. According to it, mental states are ideas which only the person having them can be aware of. Further, the mental states are essentially defined by this awareness.

This aspect of the introspectivist account seems problematic. It makes mental states essentially private, when on the contrary, the meaning of words such as `pain' is necessarily public and common to all English, who otherwise would not understand each other. Introspectivism has difficulties accounting for the fact that words like `pain' have a public meaning. it implies that I know the meaning of a word like `pain' only because of my own feelings of pain. It gives such words a purely phenomenological and private definition. By linking the definition of mental states to public behavioral criteria, the functional/causal approach avoids this problem.

However, recent writers have argued that the functional/causal approach leaves out what is essential to experience, its subjectivity. Because it omits the essential subjectivity of experience, it cannot account for subjective facts, such as what it is like to be a bat.[4]

10

Living in the Mechanical World

Am I this body? Descartes aims to show that the answer is no, because the mind and body are distinct entities. Descartes' conception of matter as an inert, dead substance, which undergoes mechanically explainable changes, makes the contrast between the physical universe and the human mind very sharp. The human mind is conscious, rational and free. Matter is dead, inert, and determined by causal laws. How can we reconcile this new conception of matter, the emerging scientific view of the physical universe, with our view of ourselves as beings who are essentially conscious and non-mechanistic?

Descartes' answer is that we cannot: therefore, the mind must be something essentially non-material. To demonstrate this, Descartes attempts to prove that the essential nature of mental substance is different from that of material substance. In other words, the new conception of matter provides proof of the existence of the soul. Properly understood, in this way, the new physics supports religion.

Descartes claims that all physical phenomena can be explained in terms of the mechanical motion of matter. However, the conscious mental states of persons cannot be so explained. A person is an essentially conscious and non-material substance or thing. Accordingly, the universe contains at least two kinds of substances: mind, whose essence is to be conscious and matter, whose essence is spatial. This position is called substance dualism. What is a human being? According to Descartes, these two distinct substances in intimate causal relations. Changes in the body constantly cause changes in the mind and vice versa.

In the Second Meditation Descartes argues that his essence is to think. In the Sixth Meditation he takes a step further towards proving dualism, by arguing that his essence consists solely in thinking. In other words, the one and only attribute without which he cannot continue to exist is that of being conscious. This new argument involves the principle that clear and distinct ideas are true, a principle that was not available to him back in the Second Meditation before he had proved the existence of God. This new argument is as follows. We clearly and distinctly perceive that in thinking of the self as a conscious being we conceive of it as having all it needs to exist by itself as a substance or complete thing. Because clear and distinct ideas are true, Descartes infers that his essence consists solely in the fact that he is conscious.

Descartes gives us three arguments for his substance dualism.

1) The argument from clear and distinct ideas

He claims to have a clear idea that he, as a conscious being, is really distinct from his body and could exist without it. He takes this to be adequate proof that the mind is distinct from the body.

2) The argument from doubt

This argument occurs in the *Discourse On the Method*, Part IV, as an application of the method of doubt:

1. I cannot doubt that I (as a mind) exist
2. I can doubt that my body exists
3. Therefore, I (as a mind) am distinct from my body.

The argument relies on the principle of the indiscernibility of identicals. This principle states that identicals, like water and H2O, must have all properties in common. If water had a property which was not shared by H2O then the two could not be identical. In more technical terms, if X is the same object as Y then any predicate, F, true of X must also be true of Y. In logical notation: $(x)(y)(F)(x=y \equiv (Fx \equiv Fy)$. Descartes relies on this principle to argue as follows: if my mind were identical with my body, then what is true of the one would be true of the other; but there is one thing which is true of my mind which is not true of my body, namely that I cannot doubt that it exists.

This argument is invalid. In the Fourth Objections, Arnauld points this out with a parallel case. I can doubt that a right angled triangle has a hypoteneuse whose square is equal to the sum of the squares of the other sides. But it does not follow that it does not have it. Another counter example is this. Water and H2O are identical. A person who is ignorant of chemistry might argue that he cannot doubt that the sea is made of water, but he can doubt that it is made of H2O, and therefore water is not identical to H2O.

Since water and H2O are identical, the argument is unsound, and so too then is Descartes' parallel argument from doubt. Why are the two arguments invalid? Because `doubt' is a psychological verb and as such is non-extensional. In an extensional context when we substitute for a word any other word that picks out or refers to the same thing, then this will not change the truth or falsity of the whole sentence. For example, `water boils at 100°C at sea level.' This is an extensional sentence because we can substitute the term `H2O' for `water' without changing whether the sentence as a whole is true. However, not all sentences are extensional. Sentences with the form `She believes that..', `He wishes that..' or more pertinently, `He doubts that..' are not extensional. They are intensional. Many inferences which are valid for extensional sentences are invalid for non–extensional or intensional ones. For example,

1. She believes that water boils at 100°C at sea level
2. Water is H2O
3. Therefore, she believes that H2O boils at 100°C at sea level.

This is not a valid argument, because `believes that' is not extensional. `Doubt' too is not extensional. For this reason, Descartes' argument from doubt fails to prove that the mind and the body are distinct. Given subjective doubt about X and lack of doubt about Y we cannot conclude that x and Y are objectively non–identical.

3) The argument from divisibility

The third argument is to be found in the Sixth Meditation. Descartes contends that he is a complete and indivisible thing. But matter, being extended, is always divisible. Hence, Descartes concludes that he, as thinking thing, must be different in kind from all matter, including his own body.

1. The mind is an indivisible thing
2. All material objects must be spatially extended
3. Anything which is spatially extended is divisible.
4. Therefore, the mind is not a material object.

Is the mind really indivisible? Plato affirmed that the soul has parts, like will, emotion, sensation and reason. Descartes denies that these are parts, `since it is one and the same mind that wills, understands and has sensory perceptions.' (AT VII 86) We can think back to Descartes' image of the wax; the wax stays the same even though it has different shapes. Similarly, according to Descartes, consciousness stays the same, even when what it does changes.

Are the following examples of divided minds? Sybil was a famous case of a person with several split personalities, many of which were unaware of what the others did. Some people have had the connection between the two hemispheres of their brain severed. In such cases, the left-hand side of the brain does not know what the right hand side of the brain is seeing (when it is deprived of the visual information, under experimental conditions). Do these examples count as having a divided mind?

Whatever the answer to these questions, there is another more serious problem with premise one, made famous by Kant. Descartes just assumes that the mind is an object. He does not consider the possibility that what we call the mind is really a property or set of properties, rather than a substance or object. Kant argues that Descartes mistakes the unity of consciousness for a unified thing or substance. According to Kant, the notion of the mind as a thing does not make sense, because the mind would have to be a non-spatial object and such a notion does not make sense. Descartes says "we cannot conceive of half a mind." (AT VII 13) Even if he is right, he does not consider the possibility that this is because the mind is not a thing at all.

Problems for dualism

Dualism is a powerful position, and certainly for reasons that Descartes understood, even if his arguments fail. By mechanizing matter, Descartes made it seem less appealing and less conceivable that we should be composed of no more than matter. The mind must be outside the clockwork order.

1) The Causal Connection

Descartes holds that there is a two–way causal interaction between the mind and the body. In sense perception neural impulses in the brain affect the mind. For instance, in seeing an object, light waves reflected from that object affect the eye and hence the brain; these changes in the brain cause us to have visual sensations in the mind. When we act voluntarily, acts of the will, which are a form of mental activity, cause physical changes in the brain which in turn cause the muscles and body to move.

Descartes was very interested in the nervous system and the brain, at a time when for many it was not even clear that the brain was the center of intelligence. His detailed anatomical studies included mapping the brain and he believed that he had located the place in the brain where it interacted with the mind - the pineal gland.

However, dualism makes this two–way interaction between the mind and the brain inexplicable. The substances, mind and matter, are utterly different in kind, and this renders interaction between them obscure, placing doubt on the whole idea of dualism. How does the mind control something which is physical, if it is not in itself physical?

This problem is more grave if the mind is a non–spatial entity, as Descartes claimed. If the mind has no location in space, then it is wrong to imagine it close to the brain. My mind is no closer to my brain than it is to the other side of the galaxy. Why then does it have a direct causal influence only on my brain? There seems to be no way of explaining why my mind cannot cause movement in your body, or in a planet the other side of the galaxy. If non–spatially located acts of will cause changes in my brain, this must be a form of psychokinesis or magic. Why is only my brain affected by this psychokinesis? Dualism cannot explain the causal connection between mind and body.

2) Neurology

Furthermore, dualism seems to contradict neurology. When particular parts of the brain are destroyed, we lose specific mental capabilities. Substance dualism cannot explain this well: if the mind and the body are two distinct things, and it is the mind which remembers, then it ought to be able to do this quite independently of what the brain does. However, in fact, when particular brain cells are killed, this will destroy particular memories.[1]

75

3) Conservation of Energy

Dualism also contradicts the principle of the conservation of energy. According to physics, the physical universe is a closed system in which total energy is conserved. If Descartes' dualism were correct, then there would be physical changes in the brain which would not have a sufficient physical cause, and this would imply denying the conservation of energy. The principle of the conservation of energy is more than just a physical law. If the conservation of energy were not true, you could not do physics. It is a necessary condition for other particular physical laws. For example, Force = mass x acceleration. If force were less than mass times acceleration, then we would have mass accelerating without sufficient force to cause it to do that. If, on the other hand, force were greater than mass times acceleration, then we would have force which is mysteriously lost, without physical effect. In other words, if the principle of the conservation of energy were not true, then F would not be not equal to MA. The same argument could be applied to other physical laws. In other words, the principle of the conservation of energy makes other physical laws possible. Therefore, the denial of the conservation of energy is a deep problem for dualism.

4) The Problem of Identity

Two material objects which are otherwise identical can be distinguished and identified as the same at different times by their position in space. Objects are publicly identifiable by their spatio–temporal position. But minds, as bodiless persons, do not have a spatial position, and thus there is no guarantee that we can identify and publicly distinguish between two similar disembodied minds. This puts into question the whole thesis that disembodied minds are substances, for substances must be publicly identifiable. If substances were not identifiable, then there would be no clear sense or content to the idea that two people were referring to or talking about the same thing. This problem is acute for Descartes who assumes that the word `I' can identify a bodiless mind. If the word `I' refers to anything, it surely must refer to an entity which is identifiable by other people. To be referred to by public words, things must have public criteria of identity. And it is doubtful that a bodiless mind can satisfy this condition.

Although Descartes argues that the mind is distinct from the body and can exist without it, he also held that in living humans there is a special close causal relationship between the two. Otherwise, the embodied person could not claim that his or her body was in any way his or hers. In particular Descartes claims that `my soul is not in my body as a pilot in a ship'. By this he means that the mind is able to move the body directly and that the mind feels pains and other sensations in the body. This will be examined in the next chapter.

Other Ontological Positions

Descartes' dualism should be contrasted with materialism, the claim that only matter and material properties exist. The materialist need not deny that we have a mind, but she must deny the existence of a non-physical mind.

However, there are other ontological positions intermediate between Descartes' substance dualism and full-scale materialism. A property dualist, for example, would deny Descartes' claim that non-material substances or things exist. The property dualist would affirm that only material things exist but would also assert that humans and other sentient beings are material things with non-material or mental properties. The property dualist would affirm: one kind of substance, two kinds of property.

In our discussion of Descartes' philosophy of mind, we have been careful to distinguish questions about the nature of mental states (introspectivism vs functionalism from chapter eight) from ontological questions (dualism vs materialism from this chapter). Although these questions are separate and are usually confused, there is at least one link between them. Some twentieth century philosophers have used the functional or causal analysis of mental states to argue for materialism. The argument has two ingredients. First, according to the causal theory, mental states are by definition whatever is capable of causing actions or appropriately complex behavior. Second, scientific neurological theory implies that, as a matter of fact, all actions and behavior are caused solely by the central nervous system. The two ingredients together imply that all mental states are brain states. In short, by definition, the mind is whatever has a certain causal role; but, as a matter of fact, the only thing which has that role is the brain and therefore all mental states are brain states. Of course Descartes would not agree to either of these two premises in the case of human mental states, and probably would agree to both of them in the case of animal mental states.

11

The Passions of the Body

Towards the end of his life, under the influence of Princess Elizabeth of Bohemia, Descartes began to think more deeply about the passions, morality and the virtues. In 1649 he wrote the *Passions of the Soul*, but his correspondence with Elizabeth also contains important discussions of these topics. He begun corresponding with her in May 1643, when she was twenty five. He wrote to her frequently, and quite intimately, and may have been in love with her, even though they rarely met. She probably viewed him as her mentor and called him "the best doctor for my soul." Poor old Descartes!

Around mid 1645, they started to correspond more frequently. From that date, she became more influential in forming his views about the nature of the passions. Descartes became more interested in the effects of the mind upon bodily health, rather than explaining health in purely physical terms. Their early correspondence, after May 1643, focused mostly on the relation between the mind and the body. Elizabeth pushed Descartes to articulate what was only implicit in what he had written before.

A Substantial Union

In his letter to Elizabeth dated 28th June 1643, Descartes refers to three primitive notions: the soul, the body and the union of the two. Descartes talks about a substantial union between the mind and body, as if the two were one substance or thing. This is because the embodied mind has very special characteristics. In this case, the whole is more than the sum of the parts.

We are embodied beings. Descartes tries to show the philosophical implications of this embodiment. It has three major consequences. First, it means that we can affect changes in nature; therefore, we have the opportunity to change things for the better. This means a responsibility to make improvements which is the key to Descartes' ethics. Conceiving of a person in terms of the substantial union is entirely different from explaining the behavior of animals in terms of their physiology. We can make changes happen. This is why we are responsible for our behavior in a way that animals are not and, for Descartes, this is a very important point for the understanding of the passions.

Secondly, it means that matter has an influence over us. It implies that we are subject to ideas caused by our bodies. These can give us a mistaken idea of how the world is; hence perceptual illusions. These ideas caused by the body make us feel as if we were located inside our bodies. Remember that according to Descartes, the conscious mind is a non-spatial substance. Yet it feels as if we are located inside our bodies. Furthermore, these ideas caused by the body subject us to passions.

Thirdly, it requires Descartes to refine, or at least supplement, his official position. The official view of Descartes is that the person is a thinking substance or a non-material and non-spatial soul. However, the human being (as opposed to the person) is a union of mind and body, with new characteristics, had by neither one on its own.

In particular, sensation and imagination occupy this curious half way position in Descartes' account of the human being. They are neither a purely mental state nor a purely a bodily state. They are characteristic of being embodied. Descartes writes:

> There are... certain things which we experience in ourselves
> and which we should attribute neither to mind nor to body
> alone, but to the close and intimate union that exists between
> (them). (art 48)

The best examples of this new class of ideas are hunger and thirst. We do not have to perceive that we are hungry and thirsty, in the way that we have to look at the dials of the gas tank of a car. Hunger and thirst are sensations we feel in our body. They arise "from the union and as it were intermingling of the mind with the body." (AT VII 81) We have them because we are embodied. Pure minds would not have them. According to Descartes, a phenomena such as hunger involves three elements: the physiological or bodily reaction; the mental judgment that one needs food; and thirdly, the special sensation of hunger. In the

Sixth Meditation, he says:

> Nature teaches me by these sensations of hunger and thirst and
> so on that I am not merely present in my body like a sailor is
> present in a ship, but that I am very closely joined, and as it
> were, intermingled with it, so that I and the body form a unit.

According to Descartes, perceptual ideas and the passions also fit
into this third category of body-mind states. The organs of the external
senses produce movements in the brain, "which cause the soul to have
sensory perception of the objects." (AT XI 346) As we have seen, these
ideas do not resemble their causes. For example, they lead us to believe
that things are colored, when nothing in the object resembles color. We
are subject to such illusions because of the bodily nature of these
sensations. This is why perceptual ideas are confused. Nevertheless,
perceptual ideas can give us knowledge of the particular things in the
world, when the ideas are properly supported and corrected by reason.

In *The Passions of the Soul*, Descartes emphasizes the dependence
of many mental functions on the body: imagination, feeling, sensation.
Of course, the more he does this, the more empty the disembodied non-
material mind seems (and the more boring the after-life seems). But, in
response to complaints that this third category does not make sense,
Descartes writes to Gibieuf in 1642:

> I don't see any difficulty in understanding on the one hand that
> the faculties of imagination and sensation belong to the soul
> because they are species of thought, and on the other hand that
> they belong to the soul only insofar as it joined to the body....

Once we remember the historical context within which Descartes
was writing, his overall strategy makes more sense. Many thinkers of
the time confused the mental and the physical, attributing mental
properties to matter to explain physical changes. In his natural
philosophy Descartes banishes all forms of vitalism. According to
Descartes, physical changes must be explained mechanically, without
any illicit appeal to purposes and mental properties (such as the fear of
a vacuum). In other words, Descartes' physics requires a sharp
separation of the mental and physical. For him, the same principle
applies to physiology and animal behavior. Mental characteristics must
only be applied to the mind as such. Only after having separated the
mind and the body, could Descartes reunite them.

The Passions

The Passions of the Soul was finished in the winter of 1645/6. It aims to give a complete account of the mind-body relation, perhaps in part replacing the planned fifth and sixth parts of *The Principles of Philosophy*, supposed to be on living beings and man respectively, but which Descartes never wrote.

Descartes was enthusiastically optimistic about the implications of his new scientific method for psychology. He was interested in the effect of moods and feelings on physical health, wanting to form a theory of psychosomatic medicine. This optimism was in part due to the fact that he thought that all biological principles must be reducible to physics. He thought his method would bring human beings many benefits, including more control of nature and better mental and physical health.

Yet it was more than that. Descartes saw the attitude of the person towards his passions as the key to a happy life. He ends his work on the passions with: "It is on the passions alone that all the good and harm of this life depends.. They dispose us to want those things which nature deems useful to us." Descartes' account of the passions forms the basis of his ethics and views on individual development.

Descartes' aim in his work is to give an account of the passions. Unlike earlier works by other authors, Descartes wants to maintain a clear distinction between the mind and the body, and not make the mistake of dividing the soul into parts. At the same time, an account of the passions must recognize that human life involves an intimate relation between a mind and a body. So whereas free will and thought belong to the mind, feelings and passions belong in part to the body. They must be explained in terms of the substantial union of the two.

Part I of the work outlines a general account of the mind-body relation, explaining the substantial union of the two and the general nature of the passions. In part II Descartes gives a classification of the passions, and in part iii, an account of specific passions and a discussion of therapeutic questions.

Descartes divides the functions of the soul into the passive and active. The term `passion' should be contrasted with `volition.' Volition is what we actively do; passion is what passively happens to us. More specifically, passions are emotions or feelings which occur in the mind because of the effect of the body.

Descartes affirms that we have six basic passions which are: wonder, love, hate, desire, joy, and sadness (AT XI 380). These six combine to form more complex feelings, such as disdain, pride, humility....For example, pride is when we love ourselves and desire to remain as we are. Anger is a violent kind of hatred, combined with a desire involving self-love (AT XI 477).

Descartes affirms that the good and ill of this life depend on the passions (AT XI, 488). He says that the sole function of the passions is to dispose the soul to will things which are beneficial to us.

Controlling conflicts

Traditional accounts of the emotions reply on the Platonic distinction between the higher and lower parts of the soul. Against this view, Descartes writes:

> There is only one soul in us, and this soul has within itself no diversity of parts (AT XI 364)

Descartes rules out the idea of conflicts between parts of the soul. If we experience conflict, it is between the body and the soul. The secret of managing these conflicts is the pineal gland, the point of contact between the body and the soul. What is required is mastery of the passions through movements of the pineal gland. According to Descartes, we can develop our will by freeing ourselves from the nervous system. Developing such freedom is essential to our becoming virtuous. But it requires that we understand the passions, which in turn requires understanding the functioning of the body.

The function of the passions is to guide us to want things which are good for us. However, sometimes the passions are an unreliable guide. They lead us to do things which harm us. Descartes does not condemn the passions for this. In fact, he thinks that this is fortunate tendency, as due to it we are forced to develop our capacity to control our emotions. Otherwise, we would merely act always on our passions and never actively will. On the other hand, when the passions are controlled by the rational soul, we can trust them in a way which does not threaten our well-being or our autonomy.

To control the passions, we need to understand how the body functions. Emotions are caused by what Descartes calls the animal spirits acting on the pineal gland, which affect the conscious mind. A passion is the animal spirit affecting the mind. In this process, we are passive. On the other hand, an act of will is when the soul causes motion in the pineal gland, which affects the animal spirits (AT XI 354-6).

Descartes' term `the animal spirits' is a little strange for us today. He thinks of the nervous system as consisting of tiny tubes through which these animal spirits move. They are entirely physical. They are physical particles, which act as messengers from the brain to the rest of the body and back again. Descartes thinks of the conflict between reason and the emotions in terms of which movements of these particles is the stronger: from the pineal control center to the body, or from the body to the pineal gland in the brain.

Because emotions are something which happen to us, the passions can be controlled only indirectly. They depend on the body. They are caused by physiological events, such as the changes in the blood and heart, which themselves cannot be directly controlled by the will (AT XI 364). Consequently, the control of the passions requires training. Descartes uses the following analogy: we cannot dilate the pupils at will but we can do so indirectly by looking into the distance.

The first step in gaining indirect control over the passions is to associate specific movements in the body with specific thoughts (AT XI 370). Like opinions, desire and passions are usually formed by habit and association. For example, in a threatening situation, a person will have certain thoughts, which will cause changes in the brain, which in turn cause a feeling of fear. Such reactions get forged over time and become a habitual link between a certain thought and a certain passion. For example, we associate the taste of medicine with a feeling of aversion. The principle of association is:

> Our soul and our body are so linked that once we have
> connected some bodily action with a certain thought, the one
> does not occur afterwards without the other occurring too. (AT
> XI 407)

Descartes' idea is that we should break old harmful associations and forge new beneficial ones, and in the process we would exercise and develop the will. Descartes compares this self-training to that of an animal. Dogs can be trained so that they sit still when they see a partridge and come towards us when a shot is fired. (AT XI 370).

The second step is to acquire direct control over desire, as an expression of free will. Passions only cause behavior via desire and through controlling her desires, a person can control their passions. In this way, a person can gain indirect control over her passions through the effect the desire has on the pineal gland. (44) Desire is good when it is founded on knowledge of good and evil. For this reason, to be able to master the passions we need to inculcate virtuous thoughts (49,170) .

Ethics

The Passions of the Body

As I mentioned earlier, Descartes' thinking about human well-being underwent a shift around the year 1645, due to the influence of his friend Elizabeth. He went from conceiving the passions in mostly physical and medical terms, to stressing the dependency of the bodily health on the state of the mind. He shifted from a physiological to a more psychological approach to well-being. For example, for treating melancholia, he advocates to Elizabeth concentrating on agreeable things, so to relax the heart and free the circulation of the blood. For example, whereas previously Descartes had thought of medicine as a way to make people more wise, in 1646 he writes:

> Instead of finding ways to preserve life, I have found another easier and much surer way, which is not to fear death. (AT iv 441) [1]

In line with this change, in part II of his last work, Descartes distinguishes different kinds of passions. Whereas the earlier part of the book concentrates on the tension between reason and the passions, Descartes now introduces a conflict between what we might call outer and inner passions. He thinks that some emotions depend more on the body than others. Pure thought can take place without changes in the body, but sensation and imagination have bodily causes and effects. Consequently, passions which involve imagination and sensation, in addition to thought, depend more on the body. Emotions which depend less on imagination, those which are more interior to the mind, will be composed solely of thoughts and they will seem like volitions. They will be free of the influence of the body. Descartes claims:

> Our well being depends principally upon inner excitations which are excited in the soul, only by the soul itself. (AT XI 440)

These inner feelings, such as intellectual joy, provide the means for the soul to find happiness within itself, without having to rely on external aid. Descartes thinks that we should cultivate these inner emotions which depend less on the body. Doing so will strengthen the will and make us less vulnerable to external harm.

These inner feelings constitute the basis of Descartes' reflections on ethics, a term which in his day included the healing of the soul. Virtue consists in always doing those things which one has judged to be best. It consists in carrying out whatever reason recommends without being diverted by passion or appetite. (ATII 371).

12
Appendix

The First Meditation sets us a sceptical challenge. The reply requires us to do two things: first, to show that Descartes' arguments for the claim that we can perceive only our own ideas are unsound, and second, to show that the claim itself is mistaken. I will very briefly present one way to do both these things, however, without arguing that these responses to Descartes succeed.

a) A problem with the two arguments

Both the arguments from illusion and from mirage assume that the content of an act of perception is the thing perceived. Effectively this means that both arguments beg the question.

To see this let us separate what the arguments collapse: the content of perception from what is perceived. On the one hand, what is perceived, or the object of perception, is a thing in the external world, which exists independently of the act of seeing. On the other hand, the content is how one perceives. For example, `I saw the *table as a brown blotch*,' the underlined words describe how one saw the table. The content of my seeing is not an object over and above the act of seeing; it is merely the way or manner in which I see. Ideas are not things seen, but seeings.

If we collapse the difference between the object and the content, then we will conclude the content of experience is a mental object.

Failure to distinguish how from what implies that we can only ever perceive ideas. It leads to treating the content of perception as a mental object, as an idea. Ideas are not what we perceive; they are the way we perceive.

Obviously a person having a hallucination is seeing, and their experience has a content. However, we should not assume that this implies that they must be seeing some *thing*. Similarly, how I perceive color can change without the object itself changing. However, this should not lead us to conclude that how I perceive is the same as what I perceive.

Specifically, in chapter 5, in argument A the second premise reads:

A2. *What I perceive* can change without any change in the object itself.

In argument B, the first premise is:

B1. *What I perceive* can remain the same, even if the external object changes or even disappears.

In both cases, the underlined phrase 'what I perceive' should be replaced by the phrase 'How I perceive'. Given this change neither argument is valid.

These points are important because the arguments put forward by Descartes seem to imply that there are private mental objects. This places us the wrong side of the veil of perception and helps create a mind-body gap.

b) A problem with the position

Suppose that we directly perceive external objects and not ideas. If we can demonstrate this, then we can overcome Descartes' scepticism. The problem with the claim that we perceive our own ideas is that it treats ideas as essentially private mental items. It treats them as things which only I (or each subject) can identify. This, in turn, requires the notion of essentially private reference. We shall use an argument based on Wittgenstein to show that this notion does not make sense.

The notion that I can identify and reidentify ideas in an essentially private way does not make sense. To show this, Wittgenstein imagines using the letter S to refer to a sensation in an essentially private way. When the same sensation returns, the person will use S again to pick it out. Wittgenstein argues that this is impossible. He claims that nothing could possibly count as the same sensation in this context.

To see why, consider how we normally identify and reidentify sensations by their public causes (e.g. the feeling of silk on your skin; the taste of cat food; a Mediterranean blue). However, this presupposes the existence of the external world. In Descartes' Method of Doubt, we are supposed to suspend belief in the external world. Therefore, Descartes is committed to the notion of essentially private identification of ideas. `Essentially private' means without any reference at all to public external criteria or causal factors.

Wittgenstein's argument against the possibility of an essentially private identification (EPI) is based on the claim that, for identification to have meaning at all, it must be possible to make a misidentification. Something must count as going wrong or making a mistake (e.g. calling a cat, `dog', or calling sensation F, `S.'). However, with the essentially private, how things seem and how things are are necessarily the same. The two necessarily coincide. Therefore nothing could possibly count as the misidentification of an essentially private sensation. We can put the argument as follows:

1. Meaningful identification requires the possibility of error
2. With an EPI, there is no possibility of a distinction between X appears to be right and X is right
3. Therefore a meaningful EPI is impossible

This argument is supposed to discredit the notion of the essentially private, which Descartes' doubt depends on. Wittgenstein's so-called private language argument challenges the heart of Descartes' position - that the immediate objects of perception are ideas in the mind.

In contrast to the notion of the essentially private, we might argue that the identification of sensations requires the possibility of public ·criteria. This means that Descartes' attempt to argue for a radical distinction the external cause and the private object of perception fails on two counts. First, it is misconceived because it treats ideas as mental entities. Instead of treating ideas as the objects of perception, we should regard them as how we perceive. Secondly, we must identify and describe the content of perception in public terms; the content of the mind cannot be divorced from the world.

BIBLIOGRAPHY

Adam, Charles and Tannery Paul, *Oeuvres de Descartes*, Paris,
    1974-86
Baillet, Adrien, *La Vie de Monsieur Descartes*, Geneva, 1970
Bloom, John, *Descartes: His Moral Philosophy and Psychology*
    New York University Press, 1978
Chalmers, David, *The Conscious Mind*, O. U. P., 1996
Chappell, Vere, ed., *Descartes's Meditations*, Rowan and
    Littlefield, 1997
Churchland, Paul, *Matter and Consciousness*, MIT Press, 1988,
Cottingham, John, Stoothoff, Robert, Murdoch Dugald and Kenny,
    Anthony, *The Philosophical Writings of Descartes*, 3.
    volumes, Cambridge, 1984-91
Cottingham, John, *Descartes*, Blackwell, 1986
Cottingham, John, ed, *The Cambridge Companion to Descartes*,
    Cambridge, 1992
Curley, E.M., *Descartes Against the Sceptics*, Harvard University
    Press, 1978
Doney, Willis, *Descartes: a collection of Critical Essays*,
    MacMillan, 1967
Durant, Will, *The Age of Faith*, Simon and Schuster, 1950
Gaukroger, Stephen, *Descartes: An Intellectual Biography*,
    Clarendon Press, 1997
Joachim, Harold, *Descartes' Rules for the Direction of the Mind*
Greeenwood Publishers, 1979
Kenny, Anthony, *Descartes*, Random House, 1968
Kolak, Daniel, *In Search of Myself*, Wadsworth 1999
Matthews, Gareth, *Philosophy and the Young Child*, Harvard

University Press, 1980

Nagel, Thomas, *Mortal Questions*, Cambridge University Press, 1979

Quine, W.V.O., *From a Logical Point of View*, Harvard University Press, 1961

Ree, Jonathan, *Descartes*, Allen Lane, 1974

Rorty, Amelie, ed., *Essays on Descartes' Meditations*, University of California Press, 1986

Russell, Bertrand, *History of Western Philosophy*, London, Allen and Unwin, 1961

Schouls, Peter A., *Descartes and the Enlightenment*, McGill-Queen's University Press 1989

Searle, John, *The Rediscovery of the Mind*, MIT Press,1994

Sorrell Tom, *Descartes,* Oxford University Press, 1978

Thomson, Garrett, *An Introduction To Modern Phlosophy*, Wadsworth, 1993

Voss, Stephen, ed. *Essays on the Philosophy and Science of Rene Descartes*, Oxford University Press, 1993

Wilson, Margaret, *Descartes*, Routledge and Kegan Paul, 1978

Williams, Bernard, *Descartes the Project of Pure Enquiry*, Pelican Books, 1978

Wittgenstein, L., *Philosophical Investigations,* Blackwell, 1953

Endnotes

Ch. 1:
[1] Roger Ariew, `Descartes and Scholasticism', in ed. John Cottingham, 1992, p. 65
[2] W. Durant,1950, p.236
[3] John Cottingham, 1986, p.22

Ch. 2:
[1] S.Gaukroger, 1995,
[2] S.Gaukroger, 1995, p. 65

Ch. 3:
[1] See D. Garber, `Descartes and Experiment in the Discourse and Essays', in S. Voss, 1993, p. 290

Ch. 5:
[1] B. Williams, 1978, p.54
[2] G. Matthews, 1980
[3] John Carriero, `The First Meditation', in V. Chappell, 1997
[4] Garber, Semel in Vita, in Amelie Rorty, 1986, p.91

Ch. 6:
[1] This section is borrowed from G.Thomson, 1993
[2] B. Russell, 1961

Ch. 7:

[1] Of course, this way of explaining it is not Descartes' own

[2] W.V.O. Quine, `On What There Is', 1961

[3] This section is endebted to A. Kenny, Chapter Ten, 1968

[4] David Rosenthal,`Will and the theory of Judgment', in V. Chappell, 1997, p.140

Ch. 8:

[1] Quoted by Daniel Garber, op. cit., p.86

[2] A. Kenny, 1968, p. 214

[3] B. Williams, 1978, Chapter 6

Ch. 9:

[1] S. Gaukroger, 1997, p.63

[2] Stephen Schiffer,`Descartes on his Essence', in V. Chappell, 1997, p.65

[3] Vere Chappell, `The theory of Ideas', in A.Rorty, 1986, p.177

[4] See, for example, Thomas Nagel, `What is it like to be a bat?', in T. Nagel, 1979; John Searle, 1994, p.93; David Chalmers, 1996

Ch. 10:

[1] P. Churchland, 1988, p. 20

Ch. 11:

[1] To Chanut, 15 June 1646, quoted from S. Gaukroger, 1997, p.388

Ch. 12:

[1] L. Wittgenstein, 1953